GETTING AND SPENDING:
The Consumer's Dilemma

This is a volume in the Arno Press collection

GETTING AND SPENDING: The Consumer's Dilemma

Advisory Editor
Leon Stein

See last pages of this volume
for a complete list of titles

THE
DEPARTMENT
STORE
Its Origins, Evolution
and Economics

H[rant] Pasdermadjian

ARNO PRESS
A New York Times Company
1976

Editorial Supervision: EVE NELSON

———◆———

Reprint Edition 1976 by Arno Press Inc.

First published 1954
Reprinted by permission of Newman Books Ltd.,
   48 Poland Street, London WlV 4PP, England

GETTING AND SPENDING: The Consumer's Dilemma
ISBN for complete set: 0-405-08005-0
See last pages of this volume for titles.

Manufactured in the United States of America

———◆———

Library of Congress Cataloging in Publication Data

Pasdermadjian, Hrant, 1904-1954.
   The department store : its origins, evolution, and
economics.

   (Getting and spending)
   Reprint of the 1954 ed. published by Newman Books,
London.
   Bibliography: p.
   1. Department stores. I. Title. II. Series.
HF5461.P18   1976   658.8'71   75-39265
ISBN 0-405-08038-7

THE DEPARTMENT STORE
Its Origins, Evolution and Economics

THE
DEPARTMENT
STORE

Its Origins, Evolution
and Economics

BY H. PASDERMADJIAN

Author of "Management Research in Retailing"

NEWMAN BOOKS : LONDON

1954

First published 1954

PRINTED AND BOUND IN GREAT BRITAIN
BY WM. BYLES & SONS, LTD., BRADFORD, 4, YORKS.

CONTENTS

CONTENTS

INTRODUCTION

THIS study was undertaken at the end of the second world war for the International Association of Department Stores with the object of providing the management of these stores with perspective for facing new problems.

It is based on one main approach, the historical approach, which on account of the nature of the subject and the aim in view, was the one most likely to reveal trends and deviations and to disclose facts in their wider relations. We think, furthermore, that, as stated by Auguste Comte, no conception can be understood except through its history.

The story of the department store falls into three clearly marked phases. The first chapter of this study is thus devoted to the formative years (1860-1880) of the department store. The second chapter deals with the next and great period (1880-1914) during which that form of distribution rose to its full stature. The third chapter treats changes which have happened during the interval of time which stretches between 1920 and 1940 and during which the previous tradition of continuous success has been gradually replaced by a new tradition of endurance in adversity. Finally, after a section which deals with the economics of the department store, we have devoted the last chapter to a survey of the future of that form of enterprise.

To sum up the object of this investigation, we may say that its aim is to find out why a form of business which during half a century had expanded with a lightning rapidity and dominated the field of retailing had, in the course of the period 1920-1940, given the impression of marking time.

In the last part of the investigation we have tried to point out the directions, perhaps distorted through the magnifying glass of our own prejudices, along which the reinforcement of the position of department stores, in relation to the other forms of distribution, might possibly be sought.

INTRODUCTION

As one will note, we have, in this last part, referred to methods or instruments of organization only in very rare instances, as the aim of an investigation like the present one is to determine what is to be done rather than how it is to be done.

We are aware of the fact that the majority of the considerations offered in these pages refer more specifically to the Parisian and American department stores, and that British department stores have on the whole avoided until now several of the exaggerations pointed out in these pages. But we must remember that Paris and the United States are the places where this institution originated, where department stores have the longest existence and have reached the most advanced stage of development. One may thus think that in their evolution during the 1920's and 1930's, they have taken a path along which they may risk to be followed by the department stores of other countries.

While we have in a few pages tried to summarize, at the proper place, the evolution of the department store during the second world war and also during the years 1945 to 1950, it must nevertheless be understood that we consider the period 1940-1950 as an interruption in the regular sequence of department store evolution. A period of prolonged seller's market caused by steady inflationary pressure can only conceal the real facts behind a façade of temporary and often only apparent profits. This is the reason why we have given so little place to the history of the last 10 years in a long-range study like the present which must refer to tendencies rather than to episodes.

The author is under a heavy debt of gratitude to the members of the International Association of Department Stores, who are at the origin of his studies in the department store field; to Mr. Derek Knee, Assistant Secretary of the Association, for his advice and constructive criticism; to Mr. W. H. Newman and Mr. A. W. Plowman who have given invaluable assistance in re-editing the original text and in submitting many helpful suggestions; and to

Miss Betty Björn for her co-operation in checking the text and reading the proof-sheets.

It must nevertheless be understood that the members of the International Association of Department Stores, in accordance with the tradition of an institution engaged in management research, have left to the writer an entire liberty of treatment. The statements made and the opinions expressed in this study engage, therefore, solely the responsibility of the writer.

I

THE BIRTH OF THE DEPARTMENT STORE
(1860-1880)

'A department store may indeed be hampered by the need of numerous checks and counterchecks, which are obstructive in many ways. But a group of men, or even a single man of great energy and insight into character, can dispense with some and make short cuts in regard to others; and so great are its opportunities in the hands of an exceptional genius, that it sometimes rises with meteor-like rapidity and splendour.'—A. Marshall.

Background

A DISTINGUISHED industrial economist once very ably defended the idea that our world has always had at its disposal the quantity and quality of inventive and promotive talent which it deserved, i.e., which it was in a position to use at that time[1]. Taking as an example the steam engine, which had been discovered, discarded and rediscovered several times from antiquity to the century of Watt, he has demonstrated that the steam engine actually broke through first towards the end of the 18th century because it was only at that time that the economic and social conditions were suitable to its application.

A similar suggestion could be made as regards the department store. One has witnessed in the course of time a number of attempts to create and operate large size retail establishments gathering different lines of trade under one roof[2]. But these attempts were short-lived, and these creations have rapidly vanished into oblivion because they were too far ahead of their time. The department store did not really appear until the middle of the 19th century, because it was only from that time on that the economic

---

[1] C. Going: "Principles of Industrial Economics", New York 1911.

[2] See examples of these attempts in G. d'Avenel: "Les Grands Magasins", Revue des Deux Mondes, Paris 15th July 1894, p. 333; H. Schliepmann: "Geschäfts- und Warenhäuser", Berlin 1913; and Fox Bourne: "English Merchants", London, I, p. 72-76. One may also mention the existence in Paris, during the 18th century, of a famous bazaar, the "Petit Dunkerque", located near the Pont-Neuf, but which was not able to develop into a departmentalized store.

conditions, themselves governed by technical developments, made the existence of the department store possible. It was thus merely one aspect of a more general transformation.

Before the 19th century the number of large towns, that is to say towns whose population reached and exceeded 100,000 inhabitants, was exceedingly limited. Moreover, on account of the non-existence of means of public transport within the towns, the inhabitants of these large cities made nearly all their purchases (not only the purchases of food or small items, but also of clothing and home furnishings) in the section of the town where they lived.

Retail stores of the specialty shop type, i.e., located in the central section of the town and which were recruiting their clientele not only in that section, but from other sections, began to appear in the largest European cities, especially in Paris and London, during the first decades of the 19th century. The same period, i.e., the first half of the 19th century, was remarkable for the introduction of a much greater degree of specialization than before within the retail stores, especially those located in the central shopping section. But these stores remained of a limited size (100 employees at the most)[3].

It is only with the development of horse-drawn buses during the following decades and the appearance of the first horse-drawn streetcars in the period 1850-1860, that the possibility of operating larger retail shops was created[4]. These retail shops of the central shopping section were able, thanks to their clientele which was drawn from every quarter of the town, to reach much higher sales volumes than the similar stores located in the other sections of the town. On the other hand, the rent charged for their sites was appreciably higher and had a tendency to rise rapidly.

[3] One may mention among these Parisian stores, which have all disappeared in the meantime, the "Diable Boiteux", the "Deux Magots", the "Petit Matelot".

[4] In Paris the horse-drawn buses appeared in 1838, but their development mainly took place during the 1850's. The number of passengers transported reached 36 millions in 1855 and increased to 107 millions in 1866 (Maxime du Camp: "Paris, ses organes, ses fonctions et sa vie", I, Paris 1873).

When this rental reached excessive levels, in fact when the rent expenses of these centrally located stores were about two or three times greater, expressed in percentage of sales, than the rent expenses of the stores located outside the central shopping section[5], there was a natural tendency for those of the centrally located shops which were expanding most rapidly to keep their rent charge within reasonable limits by extending their selling surface in depth and in height, by using for selling purposes the back of the building and also the upper floors with their lower rentals.

The economic background was thus created for larger retail enterprises selling not on one but on several floors. But these would never have had more than a few hundred employees at the most if they had continued to operate along the traditional lines of the retail trade, with one line of slow-moving merchandise, selling at relatively elevated prices.

It was by introducing in this economic background new, one may say revolutionary, conceptions that Boucicaut "invented" the department store.

The birth of the department store

In 1852, Aristide Boucicaut started in Paris, under the name of the Bon Marché, a small retail shop selling piece goods.

As regards the extent of the assortment carried, this store was similar to other shops in the trade; but Boucicaut operated his enterprise from the start according to principles which were absolutely opposed to the current practices of the dry goods trade of the time.

These revolutionary innovations of Boucicaut, a planner and a visionary, may be listed as follows:

1. While the current practice of the retail trade, especially of the dry goods trade, was to sell with a slow stockturn merchandise with a high mark-up, Boucicaut sold his merchandise at a small mark-up with the idea of compensating for the smaller gross margin by higher sales volume and more rapid stockturn.

---

[5] G. Törnqvist: "Detaljhandelns Stordriftsformer", Stockholm 1936, p. 12.

2. The current practice of retail trade was then not to mark the price of the merchandise but to permit and use individual bargaining. Boucicaut replaced this practice by the rule of offering only merchandise with fixed and marked prices, ensuring thus that all customers would receive equal treatment[6].

3. Contrary to the usual habits of the retail trade, his shop was run on the principle of free entrance. Everybody could enter the shop and look at the merchandise without that moral obligation to buy which dominated the atmosphere of other shops.

4. Boucicaut soon introduced the practice of returns, giving the customers the right to exchange the merchandise bought, or get their money refunded.

These innovations upset all pre-conceived ideas and were first greeted by the competing retailers as "du romantisme en boutique". But they corresponded to the real needs of a new age and were a striking success. The sales of the Bon Marché, which amounted to 0.5 million francs in 1852, increased continuously and reached 5 millions in 1860.

Because of this speedy development, which was the consequence of new trading principles, Boucicaut started to expand the lines of merchandise carried. He was originally handling only piece goods, but soon added dresses and ladies' coats to his assortment. He then gradually broadened the scope of his operations to include underwear, millinery and shoes. In 1863, the partner of Boucicaut became frightened of such an expansion and sold his share of the business to Boucicaut, stating: "I prefer to leave you to continue your experiments alone".

As these new lines were carried in the same store, but in separate departments, one may say that around 1860 the first department store, an entirely new framework for retail distribution, was taking shape. From 1860 to 1870 the sales of the Bon Marché expanded from 5 to 20 million francs.

[6] To understand the scope of this innovation we must remember that as late as the 18th century the distribution by retailers of handbills ("prospectus") with indication of sales at fixed prices, had been prohibited (See Martin Saint-Léon: "Le petit commerce français", Paris 1911. p. 520).

Already in 1855, inspired by the example of Boucicaut, Chauchard and Hériot established in Paris another store, the Louvre, run on similar principles, but catering for a somewhat higher income class clientele. This also expanded rapidly into a department store. In this expansion into new lines of merchandise, especially those which went beyond the clothing, apparel and textile lines, Chauchard at the Louvre soon showed himself even more enterprising than Boucicaut at the Bon Marché. It is largely under his impulse and thanks to his example that the department store quickly reached a new stage in which it covered the needs of the home, as well as clothing, by the addition of the home furnishing departments (furniture, hardware, etc.) and other classes of merchandise. These two first department stores were soon followed by other new ones. The Printemps was founded in 1865 by Jaluzot, a former department head of Boucicaut at the Bon Marché; the Samaritaine by Cognacq and his wife, in 1869.

The first country to follow the French example was the United States of America. Here there were a number of successful dry goods or apparel stores like Lord and Taylor (established as early as 1826), Jordan Marsh (1841), Lazarus (1850), Mandel (1855), Macy (1858), Wanamaker (1861), Altman (1865) and Marshall Field (1866). But all of them still confined their operation to the traditional retail lines, mostly dry goods.

The first of them to expand into department stores under the influence of the Parisian example were Stewart in New York (later absorbed by Wanamaker), Wanamaker in Philadelphia and Marshall Field in Chicago[7]. These were the stores which developed and popularized the department store in America in the 70's[8].

As stated by Nystrom, "The Bon Marché of Paris was not only the first department store, but it served as the inspiration to the establishment of department stores in all parts of the world. Stewart, Wanamaker, and Marshall

[7] J. Wanamaker: "The Evolution of Mercantile Business", Annals of the American Academy of Political and Social Science, 1900, Supplement, p. 125.
[8] J. Pyle: "Marketing Principles", New York 1931, p. 104.

Field all credit Boucicaut as the source of many of their ideas"[9].

Other stores followed rapidly. Thus Lord and Taylor added furniture and shoe departments to its dry goods business, while Macy's opened books, stationery, chinaware and silverware departments and installed a soda fountain.

Among the American department store pioneers it is probably Wanamaker who brought the most important and original contribution to the development of that new form of distribution by its rapid expansion into an endless series of new departments, and its use of advertising on a large scale[10].

The same forces which we have already noted for France were at work in Great Britain. Furthermore, it seems that the 1851 Exhibition, with its long aisles of organized presentation had opened the view of new possibilities in the methods of display and perhaps also in the classified and organized presentation of different lines of merchandise[11].

At the time when the Bon Marché and the Louvre were taking a shape which was unmistakably heralding a new form of distribution, at the end of the 1850's, there were already in operation in Great Britain some firms which have since become department stores, and whose date of foundation as retail stores was earlier than 1852. But one may say that it is in the last years of the 1860's and the first years of the 1870's that the department store started to take its real shape in Great Britain as a new form of distribution, assembling under one roof a great number of different lines of merchandise.

[9] P. Nystrom: "Economics of Retailing", New York 1932, p. 429.
[10] See the story of Wanamaker by H. Gibbons: "John Wanamaker", New York 1926; of Marshall Field by S. Ditchett: "Marshall Field & Co.", New York 1922; of Macy's by E. Hungerford: "The Romance of a Great Store", New York 1922. Filene, Lord and Taylor, and Wanamaker have also published interesting accounts of their history in the form of jubilee and other publications. Reference must finally be made to the series of articles published by G. Buchanan-Fife under the title of "Romance in the History of New York Big Stores" in the "Evening World" of New York City in July and August 1925.
[11] C. R. Fay: "Palace of Industry, 1851", London 1951, p. 91.

Here the department store materialized through the expansion during these years of the number of lines of merchandise carried by stores like Harrods, Lewis's and Whiteley's and by the creation of a special form of co-operative stores, departmentalized co-operative stores, catering for certain categories of state servants, as for example the Civil Service Supply Association and the Army and Navy Co-operative Society.

The expansion of these stores was rapid, but perhaps, in these first decades, not as rapid as in France and the United States. It seems that it is only in the 1890's that large department stores, corresponding to the size of the great stores of Paris, New York, Chicago and Philadelphia, appeared in London. On the other hand, some British provincial towns had already at that time department stores of a size unknown in the French provincial towns.

In Germany the first creation of department stores or development of existing stores into department stores began around 1880; in the Low Countries, Scandinavia and Switzerland, it started around 1890 with the notable exception of Magasin du Nord of Copenhagen which was already taking the form of a department store in the 1880's.

The department store concept also found fertile ground in the Anglo-Saxon countries of the British Commonwealth with the development of full-size department stores in Canada in the 1890's and in Australia during the first decade of the 20th century.

It must however be pointed out that to this day the department store has not acclimatized itself in Mediterranean and Eastern Europe countries, whose largest towns are still catered for by stores of a relatively small size, except in Russia, where the department stores, the so-called "Univermag", have developed greatly, but relatively late.

One may say that in the course of a few decades the department store swept across the Western world. Its success demonstrated that it represented a necessary form of enterprise. In fact, the department store can be considered as one of the most characteristic forms through which the new forces released by the industrial revolution sought expression.

It is interesting to note that the great majority of the department stores developed from a specialty shop (in most cases of the dry goods line, but sometimes of other lines, as for example Harrods which started as a grocery shop, Lewis's Limited which started as a boys' and youths' clothing store, Wanamaker which started as a men's store), and which extended their trade gradually into new lines of merchandise and thus took the shape of a department store. Of these stores which developed into a department store, one with the oldest business background is probably Steen & Strøm in Oslo, which was established in 1797. Other department stores, like the Magazine zum Globus in Zürich, have been the product of a different evolution and are the result of a general merchandise store or bazaar which has been enlarged and subdivided into departments. There are also some examples of department stores which have been created by the merger of two stores, as for example Nordiska Kompaniet in Stockholm, or which are the outcome of a store which has extended the scope of its trade by successively absorbing a number of other firms, like Stockmann in Helsingfors.

Finally a few firms, launched after that form of distribution had imposed itself, were created and started as department store firms from the beginning of their operation. Galeries Lafayette in Paris and Selfridges in London are examples.

We have shown in a preceding paragraph that the birth of that new form of distribution represented by the department store has been possible only on account of the economic and technical developments of the 19th century. But these developments have offered but the frame, the background of the stage. The department store as such has been the result of the energy and imagination of some men of exceptional ability, who had a strong sense of the needs of their time. It was their driving power, their grasp of essentials and their willingness to take necessary risks which engendered the first large-scale retail establishments. Among these men the most famous, those whose names will remain associated with the creation of the department store, are Boucicaut, who invented the department store, and

Chauchard and Wanamaker, who had a major share in
developing all the opportunities which that new form of
distribution comprised.

Competition

The only form of competition which the department
stores had to face in this first period of their existence was
that of independent retailers represented by specialty stores
handling a limited line of goods, but located, like the
department stores, in the central shopping district and
drawing, like them, their clientele from the whole area of
the town; by neighbourhood stores (i.e., stores located in
the various sections of the town and drawing their trade
from people living close at hand); and by general merchandise stores (bazaars).

The great majority of these shops were operated by
traditional and old-fashioned methods with a low rate of
stockturn (usually around one and two in the dry goods
stores) and a correspondingly higher rate of mark-up (in
many cases around 40 per cent.). Their operating expenses,
which were not large when considered in absolute figures,
were relatively high when expressed in percentage of
sales, on account of the moderate volume of the sales and
the reduced rate of stockturn. Furthermore, many of these
dry goods shops were extending credit to their customers,
with a corresponding increase in their real expenses. Besides
these specialty stores which were selling merchandise of
good quality, but at excessive prices, there were some other
shops which were selling low grade merchandise of unsatisfactory quality at low prices. The shops of either of
these two different classes were usually installed in small
quarters, their selling was largely confined to the street
floor, their merchandise was piled on shelves with no
attempt at attractive display, and they were equipped with
deep and old-fashioned fixtures.

Characteristic features of department stores during their formative years

Under these conditions the department stores had, thanks
to their commercial methods and to their very character-

istics, a marked superiority over their competitors in this
initial stage of their history.

Like the specialty shops, department stores were retail
enterprises with a central location, i.e., drawing their
clientele from the whole town. They had, however, in
comparison with the specialty shops, the advantage of
using for selling purposes the higher, cheaper floors, which
made it possible for them to be located on the most valuable
sites, while showing a lower average of rent (as a percentage
of sales) than their direct competitors. It is necessary to
point out that considerable stress has been laid on this
point by such well-known economists as Marshall, Julius
Hirsch and Törnqvist, who have dealt with the history of
the department store, and who are inclined to consider this
factor as the root of this new form of distribution[12]. Hirsch
has even, on the basis of this occupancy factor, drawn a
parallel between the development of the large industrial
plant and the department store. According to him, in the
same way as the growing size of the industrial plant is
caused by the fixed expenses which are more economically
absorbed by large-scale production, the growth of the
department store was originally caused by the possibility
of spreading the high fixed expenses of the centrally located
store (especially the high rentals of the street floor) on a
larger volume of sales obtained by the extension of the
selling premises to the cheaper upper floors[13].

Their policy of low mark-up and high rate of stockturn
allowed department stores to sell at prices which were
usually from 15 per cent. to 20 per cent. cheaper than
those of the remainder of the retail trade[14]. This mere
underselling gave them a tremendous competitive advantage. As a matter of fact, the first department stores placed
themselves from the start between the two main classes of
shops which we have mentioned in the preceding paragraph.
Instead of selling with an exaggerated mark-up first-class
merchandise or low grade merchandise with a reduced

[12] See A. Marshall: "Industry and Trade", London 1919, p. 297.
[13] J. Hirsch: "Der moderne Handel", Tübingen 1925, p. 238.
[14] Emile Zola: "Notes de travail sur les grands magasins", Collection
des Oeuvres Complètes, Tome 12, p. 474.

mark-up, they sold merchandise of good or sufficient quality with a mark-up which was formerly used only for low grade merchandise[15].

The extraordinary response which they encountered on the part of the public demonstrated that this policy answered to the real needs of the time. As a result of it their sales in several departments reached a much greater volume than those of the average store of the corresponding line of merchandise. This, in turn, allowed them gradually to get from the suppliers more favourable terms than those granted to the other retailers. One may add that their growing financial strength soon made it possible for them to secure cash discounts from the suppliers.

The department store was also characterized by the fact that it carried a far greater variety of merchandise lines than the traditional retail store. Furthermore, these different lines of merchandise were not carried in a heterogeneous assortment, as in the former general merchandise stores or bazaars, but along a new principle, with a segregation of the different merchandise lines as regards location, personnel and records in separate selling departments. Each merchandise line had a distinct location in the store, its own buyer, a separate sales force, and separate accounts were kept for it.

This basic difference between the department store and the former general merchandise store or the bazaar, has been rightly stressed by two economists in the following lines: "If you want to see a retrograde step in this progressive integration which has united under one management and under one roof numerous branches of commerce which were hitherto quite distinct, if you want to compare the modern department store with the village general shop, with its haphazard mixture of piece goods and knitwear, tinned foods and toys, drapery and stationery, then you must understand that such a comparison is valid only in terms of two stages in the evolution of an organism, like the comparison between the unformed and undistinguished chrysalis

---

[15] G. d'Avenel: "Les grands magasins", Revue des Deux Mondes, 15th July 1894, p. 334.

and the perfect butterfly with shining wings and fully developed organs".[16]

The department store thus took the aspect of a gathering under one roof of a considerable number of selling departments, each of them corresponding to a specialty shop. This feature which is perhaps the main characteristic of the department store, revealed itself, from the start, as a great force of public attraction, perhaps even stronger than the lower prices offered. It appeared very soon that that inducement to deal with other departments, which dealing with one department offers, was going to represent the most permanent asset of this form of distribution. Thus Zola noted that: "The strength of the department stores is increased tenfold by the accumulation of merchandise of different sorts, which all support each other and push each other forward". D'Avenel points out similarly: "It seems that sales breed sales, and that the most dissimilar objects lend each other mutual support when they are placed next to one another".[17]

The free entrance principle also revealed itself as a powerful asset. It gave the woman purchaser the opportunity to "shop", that is to say to go about through the various departments of a department store, or the corresponding departments of different department stores, comparing qualities, prices, styles and values to her heart's content. In itself the principle of "shopping" was not new. It was already present in the public food markets. The originality of the department store consisted in the introduction of it into fields from which it had been banished: the textile and home furnishing trades.

But it must be pointed out that neither the use of the upper floors for selling purposes, nor the collection of different lines of merchandise under one roof, is sufficient to form a department store. As reported by Michel[18] and

[16] B. Nogaro et W. Oualid: "L'évolution du commerce, du crédit et des transports depuis cent cinquante ans", Paris 1914, p. 309.

[17] G. d'Avenel: "Les grands magasins", Revue des Deux Mondes, 15th July, 1894, p. 355.

[18] G. Michel: "Le commerce en grands magasins", Revue des Deux Mondes, 1st January 1892, p. 136.

Hirsch[19], we have a number of examples of former schemes
where guilds or municipalities had grouped independent
shopkeepers belonging to different trades on the various
floors of the same building. These schemes had all been
short-lived and the groupings were incapable of developing
the vitality and efficiency of department stores because the
strength of the latter lies not only in space factors, but also
in organization factors and in an underlying unity. In
fact, the department store is not a magnified version of
the traditional retail shop, but something quite different in
kind, a closely knit organization with a new personality.

Thus the carrying of so many different lines of merchandise under one supreme management gave to the department
store the possibility of compensating for the different
seasonal peaks of the various merchandise groups from the
point of view of the use of the display windows, of the
utilization of the floor area (seasonal expansion and con-
traction of departments), and, to a certain degree also, for
the utilization of the personnel, especially the non-selling
personnel[20].

Another characteristic feature of the department store
since its inception was its wider use of the principle of the
division of labour than in any of the other forms of retailing
existing at the time. Its operation by means of segregated
selling departments did not in itself give an advantage to
the department store, as its competitors themselves operated
specialized stores carrying a single line of trade. But within
each selling department a greater degree of specialization or
division of labour was introduced, for example by the
existence of a buyer who usually devoted more time to
merchandising, travelling and buying than the owner of
the independent retail shop, and by the greater segregation and specialization of auxiliary or sales service operations
(stock-keeping, cash handling and wrapping). Finally, in
the non-selling departments the division of labour reached
a very high level. The division of labour and the corres-

[19] J. Hirsch: "Der moderne Handel", Tübingen 1925, p. 242.
[20] J. Hirsch: "Den moderne Detailhandels Hovedproblemer",
Copenhagen 1940, p. 17; E. J. B. Lloyd: "The department store as a
method of retailing", The Liverpool Trade Review, January 1953.

pondingly increased degree of organization made possible by the size of the business and the scale of the operation, allowed the department stores to avail themselves of the services of qualified specialists for the more responsible positions. At the same time, salary expenses could be reduced because the work, thus organized and standardized, made it possible to use for the lower positions, which included mainly routine jobs, less qualified personnel. It was an application in the field of commerce of the principle of delegation of skill which has been so widely employed in industrial rationalization. As a consequence of this development in department stores the proportion of women tended rapidly to become greater than that of men, whereas in former stores men had usually represented the majority of the employees.

Besides this application of the principles of division of labour and of delegation of skill, the existence of so many different selling departments allowed substantial economies by the concentration of the non-selling activities in auxiliary departments serving all the selling departments of the firm. Most activities referring to accounting, advertising, window display, credit, customers' services, delivery, store management, buying, handling of cash, etc., were carried out by central departments serving the entire store and securing thus the advantage of concentration and of production on a large scale, as compared with the specialty shops and other stores[21].

Such relative savings resulting from the large scale of the operation and the grouping of different merchandise lines in the same store are quite striking in the sphere of delivery, where the vans of the store can deliver in the same trip, often even at the same address, parcels containing purchases from several departments.

Another characteristic of the department stores has been the very alert spirit of the managers, constantly in search of new articles or very receptive to new merchandise developments, always eager to present novelties—a spirit which has

[21] See P. Nystrom: "Economics of Retailing", New York 1932, p. 161 and 163; and Törnqvist: "Detaljhandelns Stordriftsformer", Stockholm 1936, pp. 14-15.

been reflected by the very name which has been given to department stores: "Grands Magasins de Nouveautés". They prided themselves upon their ability to find and display new and unusual merchandise. They sent buyers to all parts of the world in search of remarkable articles or good values. One may say that in this aspect of their operation the department stores were reviving (or rather replacing) the mediaeval fairs. Just as in the Middle Ages the fairs handled exotic merchandise, so did the department store bring together merchandise from all parts of the world.

From the point of view of the selling transaction itself, the innovation brought by department stores was the suppression of individual bargaining, by virtue of their practice of selling at fixed and marked prices. There is no doubt that this practice, together with the policy which they followed to ensure in general that all their customers were treated alike, responded to the desires of the public and the needs of the time, and was a further element of customer attraction.

The department store also soon revealed that, by the very extent of its assortment and of the number of lines it carried, it had a distinct advantage over the remainder of the retail trade. A current practice of retailers is, as is known, to offer some products at an especially low mark-up (so-called "loss leaders"), in order to obtain a reputation for cheapness which can be spread over the whole assortment[22]. By this means they attract customers and more than compensate for these mark-up sacrifices by obtaining larger sales on goods carrying a normal or even a larger than normal mark-up. This practice is found in all forms of retailing, but it is evident that the wider the total range of goods handled by any shop, the more widely can any one price be altered without serious loss, because of the greater possibilities of finding compensation in other articles. From this point of view department stores, on account of the multiplicity of their departments and of the size of their assortment, found themselves at a distinct advantage over other retailers.

---

[22] H. Smith: "Retail Distribution", London 1937, p. 32.

In most countries the first department stores (or the former specialty shops, when they reached the stage of a department store) adopted the practice of selling only for cash, and this ensured them a corresponding saving of expenses or an additional price advantage in comparison with most of the remainder of the dry goods business, which used to grant credit to its customers.

The rate of mark-down of the first department stores was probably also lower than that of their competitors, on account of their policy of timely mark-downs and their high rate of stockturn.

The department stores undertook fairly early the organized disposal of their old stock, by means of store-wide or divisional sales events, which became a considerable element of sales promotion, while allowing them at the same time to maintain and reinforce their policy of rapid stockturn. As pointed out by d'Avenel, "One of the arts of the department stores has been to turn their losses to good account in a clever way, and to transform into a bait those articles which they have to get rid of at any price[23]".

One may say, moreover, that by paying to their executives, especially their buyers, salaries which were well above the average remuneration of retail trade executives or small store owners, and by liberal allowances for such purposes as buying trips, the department stores secured for themselves people of superior ability in choosing stock as well as the newest products and latest styles.

It has also been claimed that the department stores have had another advantage over their competitors operating smaller retail shops, inasmuch as a large firm can usually get credit from banks and financial circles more easily and at a cheaper rate than a small enterprise. However, a study of the history of the department stores reveals that this factor has not played a considerable role, as their development and growth has, in the great majority of cases, been financed by the reinvestment in the firms of the major part of the

[23] G. d'Avenel: "Les grands magasins", Revue des Deux Mondes, 15th July 1894, p. 349.

net profits made[24]. Contrary to what is the case in modern industry, the number of department store enterprises started by the resources of financial groups is very limited. It is only in the course of the 20th century, when the department store firms and concerns were already well established, that some of them have occasionally used outside capital (usually in the form of an issue of bonds) to reinforce their capacity of expansion.

But besides long-term capital there are also short-term loans, and here one may agree that department stores have often used the credit more easily granted to large enterprises for borrowing money on short-term notes and using the corresponding resources for a prompt payment of their suppliers. The operation has been profitable as they could borrow money at from five to seven per cent., while the price discounts which they obtained from the suppliers by paying cash often represented, reckoned on an annual basis, a return of from 10 to 20 per cent. on the capital thus borrowed.

It is the release of these inner forces listed which explains the extraordinary success of the department store. This success, this vertical increase of sales, was in a way revolutionary, because, as a rule, the growth of a retail firm is of necessity slower than the growth of a successful factory. Whereas a factory can reach the whole market of the country or even of the world, a store is usually dependent for its expansion upon the growth of the community where it is located. A spectacular growth such as that of the department store was therefore possible only if it deflected a growing part of the community's purchasing power from the door of competitors to its own door—a change of allegiance which, as is known, is more difficult to achieve for the retailer than for the manufacturer (where the price offered or the novelty of the articles overshadows customer loyalty or habit). The department store nevertheless succeeded; and it did so on account of two main superior-

---

[24] J. Wanamaker: "The Evolution of Mercantile Business", Annals of the American Academy of Political and Social Science, 1900, Supplement, p. 127.

ities: because it sold for less, and because it offered a greater convenience.

All the characteristic features of the department store so far mentioned refer to the difference existing between the early department stores and their competitors of those days.

It will also be of interest to consider some other characteristic features, those which refer to the difference existing between the original department stores and those of our own time.

The first striking difference lies in the operating figures.

According to the data given by Hower[25] and Zola [26], the average operating figures of department stores during this first period of their existence (1860-1880) were about as follows:—

Gross margin	.. ..	20 per cent.
Expenses	.. .. ..	15 per cent.
Net profit	.. .. ..	5 per cent.

These rates of gross margin and expenses were appreciably lower than in the period 1920-1940 and made the department store a really efficient means of distribution—one of the most economical which has ever existed.

If one seeks the main reasons for these low rates of gross margin and of expense, one is inclined to explain them first of all, paradoxically enough, by the non-existence of strong competition. At a time when the old-fashioned independent retail trade was hopelessly outranked by this new form of distribution, and when the relatively few department stores in existence were expanding rapidly and without hurting each other, both their sales promotion expenses and their customer services expenses were very moderate because they were almost superfluous.

The best sales promotion for department stores was the attractiveness of their lower prices, as well as the novelty of their new methods of distribution. Likewise the grouping under one roof of many lines of merchandise represented

[25] Report of a lecture by Ralph M. Hower, "Retailing", April 3, 1939, p. 16.
[26] Emile Zola: "Notes de travail sur les grands magasins", Collection des Oeuvres Complètes, Tome 12, p. 474.

for the customers a great convenience which acted, by itself, as the best and cheapest form of customer service.

Another general cause for a lower gross margin and expense percentage resides in the fact that in those days staple goods dominated the stock assortment of the retail trade, including the department stores, whilst fashion goods which cause a higher gross margin (on account of the mark-down risk and the higher selling and promotion expenses) were relatively much less numerous than in our day.

One may say that the early department stores of those days sold almost exclusively merchandise, and merchandise which was mainly staple merchandise. They were in a way different, not only in degree, but in kind, from the present department store which sells a complex blend of merchandise, style and service, and thus requires a more elaborate and expensive distribution process.

Furthermore, ready-to-wear and dry goods represented the bulk of their sales. We have since witnessed a great development of the home furnishing departments which necessitate, on the whole, a higher gross margin and a higher expense percentage.

The variety of different articles comprising the assortment of each department was also much smaller, before the great development of the branded article or the launching of a great number of new production lines; and, as is well recognised, the cost of distribution has a tendency to rise with an increasing variety of articles in the assortment.

The tax expenses were less because of the lower rates of taxation prevailing. The same applies to the expense items, repairs and depreciation, as a result of the lower standards of upkeep and the less rapid obsolescence of those days.

As regards the salary expenses, they represented from seven to nine per cent. of the sales and were thus appreciably lower than in our time[27].

It is true that, according to American data, the yearly sales per sales assistant were substantially inferior to those

[27] Report of a lecture by Ralph M. Hower, "Retailing", April 3, 1939, p. 16.

of our days. But this lower performance per sales assistant was partly offset by the fact that the selling staff represented over 70 per cent. of the total personnel (against about 50 per cent. in our day), and also by the lower wages paid.

Thus Hower, when comparing the operating figures of American department stores in 1870 and 1938, points out that whereas in 1870, at Macy's, the average yearly sales per employee represented $5,250 per year and the average salary paid about $5 a week, in 1938 the average salary per employee represented at least four times as much, while the average sales per employee reached less than twice the 1870 figures[28].

This great increase of the average wage, much greater than the rise in prices or the increase in sales productivity per employee, would be sufficient to explain the sharp increase of the salary expenses, considered as a percentage of sales.

The data just given refer, as already stated, to the American stores. We lack the corresponding material (especially the figures of the sales per employee) that would enable us to check whether the same evolution characterizes Europe. The salary figures that we have for the great Parisian department stores for 1880 and 1890 would tend to show the contrary, namely that the salaries and wages paid by them were relatively higher than, for example, in 1938. This would lead us to seek in another direction the cause of the smaller salary percentage of those days[29].

As regards the rate of stockturn reached by department stores in that early period, the material which is at our disposal is discordant. Zola gives an average rate of stockturn for the whole store of about four, d'Avenel of five to six, and Hower of eight. The figures of Zola and d'Avenel refer to the Parisian department stores in the period 1880-1890, while those of Hower refer to Macy's in 1888. Whilst

---

[28] See Ralph M. Hower: "Urban Retailing 100 Years Ago", Bulletin of the Business Historical Society, December, 1938.

[29] See G. d'Avenel: "Les grands magasins", Revue des Deux Mondes, 15th July 1894, p. 361; and Emile Zola: "Notes de travail sur les grands magasins", Collection des Oeuvres Complètes, Tome 12, pp. 469 and 471.

these figures are somewhat contradictory, they nevertheless seem to indicate that in those days the stockturn was higher than say 30 years later. This may, however, be explained by the composition of the trade, with its smaller relative share of low stockturn departments. It is evident that this higher stockturn contributed also to bringing about a reduction in the expense percentage of the store.

Finally, one may recall the class of trade on which the first development of the department store was based. During this opening period the department store trade was relatively more concentrated on the middle class than in succeeding years[30]. The period which ends in 1880 is, in fact, anterior to the development in the countries of Central Europe of department stores which were mainly directed towards the most popular clientele. It also preceded the creation, mainly in the Anglo-Saxon countries and in Scandinavia, of some exclusive high level stores[31].

One may say that during its first decades and under its first form the department store was mainly based on a middle class clientele. As a matter of fact, the increase in importance and in wealth of the middle class during the 19th century has been one of the factors contributing to the development of the department store.

Organization and control

The department stores of that time were usually organized on a merchandise rather than on a functional basis. They had at their head one chief executive, or a group of a few chief executives. At the level immediately below this there were no functional executives, but a few divisional or group managers, each of whom had under his jurisdiction a number of selling departments. The directing committee of the firm, where it existed, was usually composed of the chief executives and of these divisional managers. The various non-selling functions or departments (accounting,

---

[30] See C. Colson: "Cours d'économie politique", Paris 1903, IV, pp. 238 and 240.
[31] See on the Scandinavian department stores H. Raaschou: "Retailing—a Scandinavian point of view", address at the Drapers' Chamber of Trade Summer School, Oxford, 16th July, 1951.

publicity, delivery, etc.) could have at their head corresponding managers, but the latter were on a lower level than the divisional or group managers.

The methods of control concentrated mainly on the record of the sales by departments, the determination once a year (by means of stocktaking) of the gross margin of each selling department, and of records and statistics (by natural divisions) of the expenses of the whole store.

It is, however, unfair to judge these methods against the background of our present techniques of organization; for the department store represented, from its very beginning, a typical application of the principles of modern organization. From the outset, it was imprinted with the mark of efficiency. By its size, its greater degree of division of labour, its use of relatively unqualified labour welded by the resources of organization and of the principle of delegation of skill into operating teams, its preparation of events and its inventive spirit, the department store has appeared in the eyes of the public, from its inception, as one of the most tangible and striking demonstrations of the possibilities of organization.

General considerations on the period 1860-1880

When passing a summarized judgment on the department stores during the opening phase of their existence, one may say that the main reasons for their extraordinary success, for that rise without precedent, were that they ensured to the public, in comparison with the competition, lower prices and a greater service. But this greater service arose from their very characteristics (gathering of different merchandise lines under one roof) and from their business practices (free entrance, articles with fixed and marked prices), rather than from the operation of special service departments. These services were thus sources of customer attraction without being sources of increased expenses.

It may be noted that some of these elements of attraction were, so to speak, forced upon the department store by its very characteristics. Thus, as noted by C. Wright Mills, the practice of bargaining was suited only to the small store or the store of limited size. "If the entrepreneur himself does not sell, he has to have one price; he cannot trust clerks to bargain successfully"[32]. As to the principle of free entrance, it was also in a way imposed upon the department store by the gathering of several stores under one roof, which obliged a customer who intended to reach one department to pass through a number of others.

The result of this superiority of department stores over other forms of retailing was a constant and marked yearly increase in volume which, coupled with relatively low expenses, brought great net profits. These great returns were the natural reward of a more economical and more convenient instrument of distribution.

The department store has thus appeared as one of the main instruments through which the forces of a new era have sought expression.

[32] C. Wright Mills: "White Collar—The American Middle Classes", New York 1951, p. 178.

II

THE DEVELOPMENT OF THE DEPARTMENT STORE (1880-1914)

'A department store is a smoothly synchronized piece of machinery geared for volume.'
'It diversifies the temptations to buy and at the same time it concentrates the opportunity . . . If the vitality of an institution may be gauged by its architecture, the department store was one of the most vital institutions of the era 1880-1914.'—Lewis Mumford.

Background

A NUMBER of economic factors and technical developments contributed to sustain, at an accelerated pace, the progress of the department store during the period 1880-1914.

The French historian Daniel Halévy has recently spoken of eras, of times marked by the acceleration of history. One may similarly say that the period under review was characterized by the acceleration of the techniques.

The continuous and great increase in the population of the towns, especially the larger towns where the first department stores were located, was of course all-important.

But the decisive factor was probably the development of public transport. We have already seen that the birth of the department store was made possible by the development of the first means of public transport represented by the horse-drawn buses and streetcars.

Similarly, from 1880 to 1914, the great expansion of the department store was assisted, to a large extent, by the development of the electric streetcar. Thanks to its carrying capacity, relative speed and radius of action, the electric streetcar made really possible, in spite of the increase of the area and of the population of the towns, the great development of the central shopping sections. The department store profited more than any other form of distribution from this development which enabled an increasing number of people to shop away from their immediate neighbourhoods. A similar asset was represented by the development of the suburban railway lines, putting the town centre in rapid and continuous communication with its outskirts.

Towards the end of the period under consideration the development in the largest cities of underground railway and motor bus systems worked in the same direction as the electric streetcar network.

This tremendous expansion of public transport is illustrated by the following figures: In Paris the total number of passengers transported by public transport (streetcar, buses, underground railway) rose to 154 millions in 1885 and exceeded 1,000 millions in 1910[1].

Among the technical innovations which have given to the department store its now familiar aspect and without which it could not have taken its present shape, one may list the use of iron, of steel and later of reinforced concrete for the construction of department store buildings. These developments which allowed the easy construction of buildings with increased column spacings and with lightwells were particularly suited to the needs of the department store. They gave a more open view in the premises, called the attention of customers to the upper floors, and impressed the visitors with the feeling of the size and unity of this new form of distribution.

The development of the lifts likewise came in good time to solve the problem of a more intensive utilization of the upper floors. The first lift was installed at Strawbridge and Clothier in Philadelphia in 1865; the first electric lifts came to Macy's and Wanamaker in the 80's.

Other technical improvements like the introduction of electric lighting at Macy's and Wanamaker in 1878, of the telephone at Jordan Marsh in 1876, of the pneumatic tube system at Marshall Field in 1893, and of the cash register which appeared in the 80's, contributed similarly to make the operation of these great retail establishments more effective[2].

---

[1] B. Nogaro and W. Oualid: "L'évolution du commerce, du crédit et des transports depuis cent cinquante ans", Paris 1914, p. 373.
[2] W. Gabler: "Probleme der amerikanischen Warenhäuser", Zürich 1934, p. 38.

Another technical development which has had its influence on the department store came from glass manufacturing technique. While the maximum size of the window glass plates which could be produced was, until the middle of the 19th century, relatively small, the application of new processes for the production of window glass plates of greatly increased size gave the department stores an opportunity which they were the first to use, to make window display an important element of sales promotion.

During this period, one also witnessed an intensive activity in the building and rebuilding of department stores and the development of a department store architecture which has played its rôle in the creation of modern architecture in general.

Competition

The department store continued, thanks to its characteristics, to gain ground at the expense of the independent retail stores, whether of the specialty shop or neighbourhood store type. It must, however, be noted that an increasing number of retailers had been obliged, under the influence of the department store, to adopt one of its main characteristics, namely, the suppression of bargaining and the offering of the merchandise at fixed and marked prices. Furthermore, the department stores had, by their very existence, exercised an educative influence on the most enterprising retailers, especially the owners of a number of specialty shops, who started to adopt some other features of department stores, such as their attractive window and interior display of the merchandise and their policy of more rapid stockturn.

On the whole, these independent retailers did not yet represent a dangerous competition, and the department store continued to maintain its wide margin of leadership; but one could already foresee that the day would come when a relatively large number of specialty shops would, while keeping their natural advantage of a more intimate contact between the owner and the clientele, and of a sales force of a higher level, themselves appropriate several of the techniques and practices of the department store, and represent a more perceptible competition than in the past.

Moreover, in countries like Belgium, Germany and Switzerland, where department stores catered on the whole for a popular clientele and adopted a policy of rapid stock-turn and relatively narrow assortment, the specialty shops got a chance to impose themselves as firms carrying a wider assortment than department stores. In France and in the United States, the hold of the department stores on the middle class was stronger and it was mainly the highest income level clientele, always relatively limited in number, which went to the exclusive specialty shops. The development along commercial lines, in the course of the last decades of the 19th century, of the "grands couturiers" firms in Paris and in some other places also did some harm to the department stores, in the sense that a substantial part of the high income level clientele was making a number of purchases in the department stores, but was reserving its most important purchases of dresses and coats for these special firms.

Another more important competitor was brought into being by a trend evoked by department stores themselves. By the development that the latter had given to the sales of ready-to-wear clothing they had contributed to shift the centre of gravity of the clothing business in general from piece goods to ready-to-wear. The growing habit of the feminine clientele of buying ready-to-wear clothing gave birth to a substantial number of ready-to-wear specialty shops which often revealed themselves in a better position to compete with department stores than the former piece goods stores.

One must likewise note the creation of large, department-alized, specialty stores which were in fact department stores without a home furnishing division.

But on the whole it is possible to assert that the department store during this period was still keeping its initial advantage over the specialty shop and the independent retailer in general, as these traditional forms of retailing were still too much dominated by old-fashioned methods and conceptions, whilst the department store was still vibrant with the vital force which originated it.

The free entrance principle and the whole atmosphere of department stores contributed to make more and more of them pre-eminently shopping stores. It is in this period that they secured so much of the shopping trade (the trade which involves a careful comparison of price, style and quality), that the smaller dry goods stores abandoned this trade in increasing numbers and confined themselves to a large extent to the selling of convenience goods (goods bought without shopping or comparison between several stores).

The competition from other, new forms of distribution was negligible. The mail order business developed either, as in America, through the medium of firms which were mainly covering an agricultural clientele or, as in Great Britain and France, through the medium of the department stores themselves. The chain stores were still at the beginning of their existence, and they concentrated their activity almost exclusively on the food lines where the department store was not, or only very slightly, represented. As regards the unit price stores or variety chains, they existed only in the United States and confined their operation in those days to the sale of five and ten cent articles, i.e., articles which represented a very small proportion of the assortment of the department store and the sale of which was probably considered as a nuisance[3].

One may say that during this whole period the total volume of retail sales in the towns where department stores were located increased substantially and almost continuously, on account of such different factors as the increase of the population of the towns, the existence of a long period of relatively continuous prosperity, the rapid

---

[3] As a matter of fact, even in America, the development of the chain store and of the unit price store took place later than is commonly imagined. In spite of the fact that the Great Atlantic and Pacific Tea Company established its first store in 1858, and Woolworth in 1879, the corresponding chains started to gain momentum only in the period 1900-1915 and their great expansion took place in the period 1915-1930. See D. Bloomfield: "Trends in Retail Distribution", New York 1931, pp. 223-224.

growth of factory production and of selling through retailing of a number of textile and other goods (ladies' ready-to-wear, underwear, millinery, laces, embroideries, etc.) formerly made in the home.

This continuous increase of the total retail sales volume would have been sufficient in itself to ensure a continuous rise in the sales of department stores. But the sales of department stores expanded at an even higher speed, because the latter ensured themselves an increasing share of the total retail sales. In fact, the gauge of the strength and vitality of a form of distribution is not its ability to increase its sales volume in absolute figures, but its capacity to increase its sales at the cost of the share of other forms of retailing.

This relative progress of the department store was due to the reinforcement of the position of the stores located in the central shopping section, thanks to the development of the means of public transport, as well as the extraordinary attraction exercised on the public by the department store, which was imposing itself as the most attractive and economical form of retailing.

Indeed, the most important competition with which department stores had to cope in the latter part of that period was probably not represented by other forms of retailing, but was already found in the department store line itself.

The purchasing power of the population at this time was lower, even in relation to the lower cost of living, than in our time, but most families had more available money at hand than in our days. This was due to the fact that it was a general habit to live within one's income. Furthermore, many of these families had at their disposal the accumulated savings of former generations.

Unused purchasing power was therefore present in the hands of the public. What was lacking was the habit of spending. And it was here that the department store with its methods, especially its technique of window and interior display, its concentration of the buying opportunities and its use of sales promotion, played a major rôle in inducing, one may almost say educating, the public to buy. The great increase in the sales of department stores during this period is thus not only due to their encroaching on the turnover of other forms of distribution, but also to the fact that they induced in a great number of people the habit of spending more, and thus put into circulation, in the form of purchases, an appreciable proportion of the money which had previously been saved.

It was due to the existence of this considerable reserve of unused purchasing power among the public that all the initiative that department stores applied to the increasing of their sales met such a ready response.

*Characteristic features of department stores during
the period of their great expansion*

The history of the department store during the interval of time which stretches between 1880 and 1914 is proof of their capacity to rise to the level of their opportunities. This period corresponds to the great expansion of the department stores, the period in which this new form of retailing rose to its full stature, some of these enterprises assuming even the character of national institutions. This development without precedent has been the best proof of the useful rôle played by this new form of distribution. As noted by Mazur, "The department store would not have grown unless it was basically sound internally as well as in its relationship with other units of the economic chain"[4].

It was also during these years that the department store started to exercise a major influence on the whole field of retail distribution. While department store sales have always represented a relatively limited percentage of the total retail sales of the various countries, one may nevertheless say that this new form of distribution was making the pace and setting the tone for the rest of retailing.

The main characteristic features of the department stores during this period were, on the whole, the same as those we have listed in a corresponding paragraph of the preceding chapter and which have given to this form of distribution its peculiar shape.

---

[4] P. Mazur: "Principles of Organization applied to Modern Retailing", New York 1927, p. 2.

But beside those main characteristics of the department store which remained unchanged during the period under consideration, we can trace other forces, some of which were already at work in the former period, but all of which have really consolidated themselves only after 1880.

In the course of this rise to maturity the department store continued to expand into new lines of merchandise by the creation of new selling departments. Here again the department store showed its great vitality by its extraordinary power of expansion. It incorporated gradually the products of the most various fields of human activity. However, department store experience soon showed that if it could become a universal provider it could not come to mean all things to all men. Department store men became convinced, after having harboured some illusions, that even the greatest department store is obliged to select a given income group (high, medium or popular) for its clientele and to adapt its assortment and its operation to the needs of that income group.

The dynamic vigour of the department store, disrupting the former structure of retailing, produced an innovation which deserves to be recalled here. When the department store started to penetrate into new lines of merchandise, it usually adopted them as they were established in the retail trade. That is to say it had a silk department, a chinaware department, etc., corresponding to a great extent, by the composition of their assortment, to the specialty shops existing in those lines, with a grouping of the merchandise according to its origin.

In the period under consideration, however, the department stores, using the opportunities afforded by the multiplicity of the lines of merchandise that they carried, started (somewhat timidly, it is true) a few innovations by the development of some selling departments of a new type, i.e., which had no counterpart in the retail trade, and where the merchandise was grouped on the basis of related needs, selling those articles that the customers use or buy in association (for example the men's underwear and accessories department). As is known, this innovation has been followed by the remainder of the trade and has given birth to specialty shops of the corresponding types.

It is also during this period that the display technique of department stores, both in windows and in the interior of the store, made great progress. The department store became more and more an institution, a centre of attraction, and one may also say a kind of permanent exhibition.

Some department stores developed also a considerable mail order business, for example those of London and Paris which made up to 25 per cent. of their sales through this means.

Finally a number of department stores started to open and operate their own production and manufacturing units, with the main purpose of reducing the purchase prices of the articles, but in some cases also to obtain exclusive merchandise or to satisfy the demand of their customers for articles not found on the market.

But besides the features which we have just listed, the period from 1880 to 1914 was characterized by a number of others, of a greater importance, because they have had a stronger effect on the evolution of the operating figures of department stores.

Among these we must first point out the use on an increasing scale of sales promotion represented by advertising (in newspapers and by catalogues). These activities were already present on a small scale from the very birth of the department store, but they reached a size where they began to appear in the expenses of the stores only from this time on. The Parisian department store had used advertising very early in its career, and the first full page advertising insertion of a department store appeared as early as 1867; but it was mainly Wanamaker who, thanks to two imaginative and resourceful advertising managers, Powers and Gillan, gave a decisive impetus to the use of advertising in the form of newspaper insertions, by the department stores[5]. D'Avenel quotes the publicity expenses

---

[5] W. Gabler: "Probleme der amerikanischen Warenhäuser", Zürich 1934, pp. 40-41.

of the Parisian department stores as having already reached two per cent. of sales by 1893[6].

If one tries to seek the reason for this development of the publicity budget, one is inclined to attribute it partly to increased competition, more especially to competition between department store and department store.

But this growing use of advertising was probably mainly due to certain characteristics of the department store as a form of distribution. It appeared very soon that the consolidation of so many merchandise lines in the same store allowed an economy in the use of advertising or an increase of its effects, which placed the department store at a distinct advantage over other retailers in the use of advertising and sales promotion in general. One must also consider that (as earlier noted) this was still a time where there was an appreciable amount of unused purchasing power in the hands of the public—a situation in which the response to publicity is relatively very great.

Furthermore, the larger use of advertising by department stores has also been a consequence of the lower level of skill in their personnel, when compared with the better selling personnel of the specialty shops. As noted by Nystrom: "The department store uses its advertising to secure customers. In a measure it substitutes skilled advertising for skilled salesmanship"[7].

Another item of expense not included in the publicity budget, but which was nevertheless a sales promotion expense, and which increased continuously during this period, was the one represented by the service departments and customer services.

The development of these service departments and customer services was due mainly to the competition which developed between department stores themselves. It contributed strongly towards the attraction exercised by the department store as a form of distribution, and reinforced the department store's hold on the public—at the cost,

[6] G. d'Avenel: "Les grands magasins", Revue des Deux Mondes, 15th July 1894, p. 365.
[7] P. Nystrom: "Economics of Retailing", New York 1932, p. 165.

however, of an increase in its gross margin and expense ratio.

Other new features of the department stores were represented by their further penetration into the fields of home furnishings and a number of other lines; and this likewise probably helped to increase their gross margin and expense ratio.

The growing proportion of merchandise dominated or affected by the fashion factor, as well as the ever-increasing variety of articles entering into the composition of the assortment of the various departments, have also their responsibility in the increase of the gross margin and of the percentage of expenses. The development of the ready-to-wear business at the expense of the piece goods sales is another factor making for increased expenses.

Yet another reason for the increase in the gross margin and expenses resided in the fact that the department store, while remaining a retail firm, has tended, by its buying and merchandising methods, and thanks to its purchasing capacity, to short-circuit the wholesaler, the commission house, the jobber, and the importer, and to establish a direct connection with the manufacturer or the great wholesale distributor. It is, for example, well-known that department stores are less inclined than other types of retailer to wait for the salesmen to come to them with their offers. Most department store buyers go direct to the manufacturers. But this point is only a secondary illustration of the fact that the department store, by its methods of work and the extent of its field of operation is substituting itself for the usual wholesaler. The department store does not represent an exclusively retailing enterprise, but to a certain extent an integration of retailing with wholesaling, and in some cases even with manufacturing. It performs operations such as storing, financing and assembling, normally performed by the wholesaler in the ordinary process of distribution. This evolution has brought to the department store the advantage of lower purchase prices. On the other hand, the department store was obliged to replace the former wholesaler and to perform some of his functions, with a corresponding increase of expenses. As stated by

Professor McNair, "The department store has partly absorbed the wholesale function; its gross margin reflects this. The increase of the cost of doing business of the department stores can be partly attributed to the cost of functions transferred to them from other sections of the distribution system"[8].

The growing size of the department stores, the increase in their administrative apparatus, the growing refinement of their internal structure have probably also made their contribution to this trend of rising expenses. One must, however, consider that this growing size of the department store gave them an increasing opportunity of fulfilling one of their main missions, that of applying the principles of large-scale production to the problems of retail distribution. We are furthermore of the opinion that, if the expenses represented by the service departments and especially the customer services (expenses which are drowned in the various functional divisions) were carefully segregated, one would find that the increase of the real administrative expenses of department stores (expressed as a percentage of sales) in the course of their history, or concurrently with their increase in size, is much smaller than is commonly imagined.

This is not without its importance. When the department store began to expand it was commonly thought, on the basis of industrial experience, that the increase in size of the department store was going to be accompanied by a decrease in its expense percentage and in its cost of distribution. The evolution which actually took place between 1880 and 1914, a period during which department stores enormously increased their sales, but also saw an increase in their rate of mark-up and gross margin, led many observers to the conclusion that department stores, unlike industrial firms, saw their costs of distribution increase with their size, probably on account of ever-increasing administrative expenses. But this conclusion is not supported by actual evidence. The statistics at our disposal seem to show that the purely administrative expenses of

---

[8] M. P. McNair: "Trends in large-scale retailing". Harvard Business Review, October 1931.

department stores (expressed of course as a percentage of sales) have a tendency to decrease with an increase of the size of the store, and that it is other expenses, mainly the occupancy, the advertising and the delivery expenses, which show an increase with a growth in size of the department store.

All the factors reviewed tended to increase the expense percentage of department stores. Their effect was, however, partly counter-balanced by two positive factors: (1) the continuous and great increase in turnover; and (2) the increasing strength of the department store in relation to the suppliers (wholesalers and manufacturers) who granted them special purchase terms (lower prices), either because of the scale of their purchases or of the standing and reputation which made department stores desirable channels of distribution likely to enhance the prestige of the products handled.

It is the combined action of these factors which has resulted in an evolution which is expressed by the following figures:

While in 1880 the average gross margin of department stores was in the neighbourhood of 20 per cent., in 1914 the average gross margin had reached the neighbourhood of 30 per cent. As regards the expense percentage it passed during the same period from about 15 per cent. to 25 per cent.

We have no reliable figures on the evolution of the rate of stockturn during these years, but are inclined to believe that this figure showed a downward trend during that period.

Appearance of department store chains

At first, department stores were established and operated only in large towns, i.e., towns with a population of at least 100,000 inhabitants. During the first decade of the 20th century department stores started to appear in smaller towns. The prestige gained by this form of business, a certain local vanity, the spirit of emulation, all played their part in the foundation of these firms.

It soon appeared, however, that the independent department store located in a small town had a number of disadvantages compared with the department stores located in a large town. We have already stated that it was the high and exaggerated rentals of the central shopping district sites of the large towns which contributed to the creation of the department store, i.e., a store using for selling not only the street floor, but also the cheap upper floors. In the large towns, on account of the high rentals, the department store had thus a distinct advantage over the other stores. In the smaller towns, where the rentals of the best locations do not reach such an extreme level as in large towns, the relative advantage of the department store form of business, as regards occupancy expenses, was less pronounced.

Another, more serious handicap of the small department store resided in the fact that the great advantage of the department store, viz.: the more favourable purchase terms its large orders could command, could not be obtained by stores located in the small towns.

Some of these department stores tried to increase their sales volumes by broadening the width of their assortment, i.e., by carrying goods which answered the needs of high, medium and low income class clienteles. But this policy soon revealed itself as a serious handicap by the increased complexity of the stock which had to be carried[9].

It thus became evident that there existed a downward limit to effective department store operation, and that this downward limit is set by the smallest scale upon which the store can purchase economically.

The consequence of such experience was that small department stores operating in smaller towns tended more and more to take the form of branches of large department stores or units of department store concerns, operated in different towns, but under a common management, and in some cases with a common buying organization.

This development of chains of department stores was, however, not confined to small-scale branches of a great

---

[9] H. Smith: "Retail Distribution", London 1937, p. 50.

department store, but included also the establishment of chains grouping only (or mainly) large-size department stores.

Organization and control

The organization structure of department stores in Europe during this period remained, on the whole, dominated by the merchandise rather than by the functional principle; but one witnessed a reinforcement of the relative position of some functional executives, bringing them in some stores to the level of the group managers.

In America, the position of some of these specialized functional managers (the controller, the advertising manager and the store manager) became relatively stronger, and they gradually found themselves on a level which was exceeded only by that of the general manager and of the merchandise manager.

Furthermore, the period 1910-1920 was characterized in America by the development of the personnel function and the creation of training departments in various stores.

In the field of the methods of control the main instruments remained on the whole the same as previously, i.e., the control of the operation of the department store was based mainly on the possession of the following figures: the sales per department, the gross margin per department available at the end of the year after stocktaking, and the records and statistics, according to natural divisions, of the total expenses of the store. Here and there some items of expenses representing functional divisions (especially those referring to non-selling departments) began to appear, but without an attempt to separate them clearly from the natural divisions of expenses.

One may say that on the whole department stores continued to be organized and operated along the same lines as in the preceding period. The difference was one of emphasis rather than of method. Moreover, during this time of growth the problems of expansion overshadowed those of organization. Those who lived in the atmosphere of this stupendous advantage, especially towards its end, came to take it for granted, with a corresponding contemptuous disregard for research.

Thus at the end of this period we had the department store, we had to a certain degree even organization, but we had not yet research in the sense of specialized and organized knowledge.

General considerations on this period

As we have seen, the cost of distribution of the department store increased markedly during the period under consideration, which goes from 1880 to 1914.

At the end of this period of unexampled expansion, i.e., around 1914, department stores were still at an advantage, as regards selling prices, compared with the other forms of distribution, but this price advantage was not as great as in former days. Furthermore, it was no longer the result, as before, of an expense percentage appreciably lower than that of the other retailers, but rather the consequence of the more favourable purchase terms secured from the suppliers, thanks to the great sales volumes reached in several departments; often also by the mere force of prestige.

We have stated in the preceding chapter that during the period of their birth (1860-1880) the continuous and extraordinary increase of the sales of the department stores, their winning of customers from the other forms of distribution, were due to two underlying causes: they sold for far less than the other forms of distribution, and they rendered greater service to the customer.

During the following period of 1880-1914, the continued development of the sales of the department stores was due to the same causes, to which one may also now add a third: sales promotion.

Department stores were on the whole still cheaper than their competitors, but the price difference was probably not as great as before (on account of the growing expense of department stores and also of the tendency of the competitors to imitate their pricing policies). On the other hand, the advantage of the department stores as regards greater service rendered had become even more marked than previously. The old advantage of greater convenience to the customers by the grouping of many lines under the same roof was retained, while the development of a great number of service departments and customer services had increased the conveniences extended to the customers.

Finally sales promotion under the form of advertising has appeared as an important tool of sales building. It was very soon found that department stores, through their size and their characteristics, were in a position to use advertising more economically and more effectively than any other form of retailing. This increase of advertising probably shares with the development of the customer services the main responsibility for the increase of the expense percentage of department stores during this period.

But it is thanks to these efforts that the department stores were able to maintain their continuous and marked yearly sales increases. As the expenses represented by the services to customers and the sales promotion had not yet reached extreme levels, and as the response from a market which was not yet saturated was on the whole more ready than in later periods, one may assume that these efforts were profitable and that their results still exceeded their costs.

The phenomenal expansion of the department store during this period was the best proof of the fact that it corresponded to a powerful economic need. It has achieved a very important place in the economic process. As noted by Nystrom, it has become as much a part of modern civilization as rapid transport, the use of electricity or advertising and (one may add) the daily newspaper[10], all of which were also in themselves essentials to department store development[11].

We have already stated that in the eyes of the public the department store, whatever its shortcomings when judged

---

[10] In fact, the development of the large daily newspaper has taken place concurrently with the expansion of the department store, and one may say that either of these modern economic and social instruments would not have reached its present stature without the existence of the other. The total circulation of the Parisian daily newspapers increased from 100,000 in 1834 to 1,500,000 in 1877, and exceeded 4,000,000 in 1914.

[11] P. Nystrom: "Economics of Retailing", New York 1932, pp. 155-156.

against the background of modern management principles, represented one of the most striking examples of application of the science of organization.

Likewise economists greeted the department store as the embodiment of the great forces which dominate modern business. "The department store is the most marvellous illustration of the great directing principles of modern economic life. Specialization, concentration and integration are all united there, without these apparently contradictory tendencies excluding each other in any way"[12].

The era which stretches from 1880 to 1914 will remain the greatest period in the history of the department store. One can say that during a period of nearly 40 years the department store really sailed on the top of the wave, maintaining undisputed sway over the field of distribution. At the same time, its example initiated forces and created conditions which have given a new shape to the whole retail trade. The department store has, in fact, stamped its mould on distribution and has become the standard of measurement by which all other forms of retailing, old and new, have surveyed their methods of operation.

The department stores during the first world war

We have devoted this chapter to the period extending from 1880 to 1914 because it was a convenient interval of time to use, without any marked breaking-point between these two dates. But it is plain that this period really extends to 1920 and thus includes the great convulsion of the first world war.

These years of war have been characterized, as have all similar periods, by the existence of pronounced seller's markets brought about by the great increase of the money in circulation, the continuous rise in prices and a certain scarcity in goods.

The consequence of this situation has been for the business world in general, including the retail trade and department stores, a great increase of sales and net profits. The great profits of this period were caused not only by

---

[12] B. Nogaro et W. Oualid: "L'évolution du commerce, du crédit et des transports depuis cent cinquante ans", Paris 1914, p. 308.

the ever-increasing sales, but also by the rise in the prices of merchandise which allowed department stores (as all business) to make, beside the profit resulting from the usual operation of their firms, substantial profits deriving from the increase in the value of their inventory. As price control stipulations were at that time much less developed than in the second world war, and the incidence of taxation was still relatively small, the net profits of all lines of business, including department stores, were very great.

As, however, the first world war represented an absolutely new experience, and as both the sales increase and the rise in prices continued after the war, at least during the whole of 1919 and part of 1920, business circles failed to appreciate the exceptional character of the circumstances and continued to build up stocks as if this extraordinary situation could continue for ever. Inflated by their sweeping but easy successes they ignored the real mission of their profession, which is service and not speculation. When in 1920-21 the inevitable reaction came in a relatively short but violent world crisis of price deflation, with a steep drop in values, most business enterprises, including department stores, were caught off their guard, with exaggerated stocks. The great loss which they had to cover on the sudden reduction of the value of their stock wiped out in most cases a substantial part (if not the whole) of the financial reserves they had built up during the exceptionally favourable years between 1915 and 1919, and even brought some firms to the edge of ruin.

III

THE EVOLUTION OF THE DEPARTMENT STORE DURING THE PERIOD 1920-1940

Background

THE major technical development of the period 1920-1940, between the first and the second world wars, was the great expansion of motor transportation.

As a means of public transport, in the form of motor buses, it extended the mobility of the population within large cities and increased the importance of smaller cities as retail centres by allowing the country population to visit them more easily.

As regards privately owned automobiles, the multiplication of their number has not exercised any marked effect on the shopping habits of the town population (if one excepts some American developments, especially found in California, which refer to special conditions). On the contrary, the growing traffic congestion in the central area of large towns, resulting from the great increase in the number of automobiles in circulation, has had on the whole a detrimental effect on the growth of the central shopping district of the largest cities. The department stores of these largest towns have been affected by this situation, but perhaps less than the specialty stores, since these traffic difficulties have, within the central shopping section, stressed the convenience of a firm where the shopper can complete his different purchases without leaving the store.

The smaller growth of the total population of the large cities during this period, and the shifting of part of the population from the central area to the suburbs, have also contributed towards slower sales increases for the retail trade in general, and especially the centrally located retail trade.

On the other hand, an auxiliary factor, the development of the escalator, has represented for the department store a distinct asset. We have already stressed that one of the characteristic features and economic factors of the department store was always that extension of the selling area to the cheaper upper floors which gives to the department store an advantage as regards rental expenses in relation to its competitors, especially the specialty stores located in the central shopping area. But the attraction of customers to these upper floors has always represented a most difficult problem. In former days the existence of a lightwell and of open staircases helped in tempting customers to visit the upper floors of a department store. But this element of traffic attraction has had a tendency to disappear on account of the growing suppression of the lightwell and the replacement of open staircases, i.e., staircases in free connection with the selling areas, by stairways enclosed in fire-resisting walls. As even the multiplication of the number of lifts has revealed itself incapable of remedying the effect of this transformation, one may say that the development of the escalator represented a welcome addition, apt to reinforce that use of the upper floors which is one characteristic and economic advantage of department stores.

The great development of the moving picture as a form of entertainment must also be recorded as another auxiliary factor influencing this period. One may say that this influence has, on the whole, been not unfavourable to department stores. It is known that one of the missions and aims of department stores has been to stimulate the buying desire of the public and to create and direct buying habits by means of their advertising, their displays and events; and in this process the moving picture has revealed itself as a useful and inexpensive auxiliary, in inducing people to visualize new styles in home decoration and equipment, clothing, personal appearance, etc.

As regards the general economic conditions prevailing, the years from 1920 to 1940 may be divided into three stages. In the first, from 1920 (or rather 1922) to 1930, thanks to the expansion of money circulation which took place during the first world war, to the work of reconstruction and re-equipment which was necessary (especially in the building trade) and to the credits allowed by the Anglo-Saxon countries, the different countries enjoyed a period of relative prosperity, during which the effect of the ill-balanced economic structure left by the first world war could be hidden for a while. This defective economic structure was itself the result of a number of factors, such as the over-expansion of many industries, the industrialization of overseas countries, a general and excessive economic nationalism, prohibitive customs duties, and increased rationalization favouring the accumulation of capital and the expansion of the production facilities, rather than an increase in the purchasing power of the population.

A time had, however, to come when the consequences of this ill-balanced economic structure and system were to be felt. They produced from 1930 to 1934 a violent and long depression, perhaps unique in its magnitude and length. Retailing, like most other branches of human activity, was shaken by the storm of an unprecedented crisis[0]. In the United States and Germany (which were, it is true, the countries most violently hit by this depression) the fall in retail sales between 1929 and 1933 was respectively 49 per cent. and 41 per cent.

During the third period, from 1935 to 1939, the world enjoyed a relative recovery; but this was due to artificial measures such as large-scale public expenditure and the armaments race, rather than to a real cure by the suppression of the factors which were the cause of the evil.

Finally, a few words have to be said on a general experience of these last decades. The reduced cost of production achieved by technical development, rationalization, mass production, etc., had no counterpart in distribution, but on the contrary was accompanied by an increase in the cost of distribution cancelling out much of the advantage of mass production. This phenomenon is due partly to the fact that in industry output per man has been steadily increased by means of technical progress and mechanical equipment, whilst in distribution the output per man, or average sales figure per sales person, has remained much more constant, in a field where technical developments play a secondary rôle.

Another cause of this paradoxical relationship between low-cost production and high-cost distribution lies in the fact that in the period between the two world wars the purchasing power of the population did not increase in

[0] E. Steen: Address to Oslo Commercial Assoc., Nov., 1934.

proportion to the growing output of an industry geared for mass production. Left to itself the market would have absorbed only a portion of the great mass of goods supplied by industry. In order to increase the capacity of absorption of the markets, what may be called artificial methods of stimulation, such as increased advertising, high pressure sales promotion and greater service to customers, have been adopted. These have been able to increase consumption, but only at the expense of a higher cost of distribution; and this increase in the cost of distribution has offset much of the price economies of modern mass production.

This situation is not peculiar to department stores, as it is a general trend which has affected the whole retail trade, not to say the whole economic system of various countries; but it was perhaps nowhere more clearly reflected than in the operating figures of department stores.

Competition

From the point of view of competition one may estimate that the period 1920-1940 marks the beginning of a new era in which in many countries the department stores, considered as a whole, no longer increase their relative share in the total retail sales of the towns in which they operate, but just hold their own or even witness a decline in their relative part in the total volume of retail sales.

This situation is due partly to the reinforcement of some forms of distribution and to the development of new ones, partly to other factors.

Among the older forms of distribution one may note that an increasing number of specialty shops, influenced by the stimulating example set by department stores, have adopted some of the latter's most successful features, especially as regards methods of merchandising, sales promotion and display. We have even witnessed some bold innovations on their part (as for example the Champs Elysées dress shops in Paris, or the "Guinea" dress shops in Great Britain, selling at unit prices). Thus a form of retailing which had been for years a pupil of department stores showed an inclination to start experimenting and thinking for itself, upon its own lines. As regards the services extended to customers, specialty stores, without going as far as department stores, and thus avoiding some of their exaggerations, have extended the services offered to their customers.

In the meantime, the relative advantages that the specialty stores have always had over department stores have remained. The main advantages here are, as is known, the more direct contact of the owner or manager with the personnel and the clientele, the higher quality of the sales force, a clientele more restricted from the point of view of income class differences than that of the department store and whose needs are therefore easier to meet, even though these customers may be on the whole individually more exacting. The growth in number, in size, and in competitive strength of specialty stores, especially in the men's clothing and accessories and women's ready-to-wear lines, is one of the characteristics of these decades.

The increased competition from the specialty shops which we have just outlined was largely the result of an imitative development. Another important factor which has served to reinforce the position of the independent retailer in general is the growth of nationally advertised brands and of the practice of price maintenance (i.e., uniform resale prices dictated by the manufacturer).

Besides this reinforcement of the specialty shop or of the individual retailer in general as a result of the teachings of the department store, and of the growth of national brands, another source of competition has appeared in new forms of distribution, mainly represented by the specialty chain and the unit price store or variety chain.

While until the first world war chain stores were mainly developed in the food (especially grocery) line and, in the United States, in the drug store line, during the period under consideration the chain stores selling clothing and home furnishing lines have achieved, especially in Great Britain and the United States, substantial expansion, and have started to represent an appreciable percentage of the total sales of these fields, mainly in the lines of shoes, men's clothing and accessories, ladies' ready-to-wear, dress accessories, underwear, hosiery, millinery and hardware. Some of these chains are operated by manufacturers as outlets for their products, others are purely commercial firms.

All these fields are in direct competition with the most important stock lines of department stores. The growth of the ladies' ready-to-wear chains has represented a special menace, so much the more in that, whilst wearing apparel chains previously dealt nearly exclusively in staples, they have started to handle, not without success, fashion goods, i.e., a type of merchandise which was formerly believed to be too difficult for chain operation.

On the European Continent these specialty chains have not yet arrived at the proportion attained in Great Britain and America; but they are nevertheless rapidly gathering momentum, and have already reached real development in a few merchandise lines—as, for example, the ladies' underwear and hosiery chains in several European countries, the shoe chains in France, Germany and Switzerland, the men's clothing chains in France, the Low Countries and Switzerland. Their success has been great, and they represent a warning for the future, provided that legislative restrictions do not hinder their development.

As is known, the strength of these specialty chains resides mainly in their great buying capacity, their technique of selecting the items carried, the greater merchandise specialization of the management, their very modern methods of merchandising, their selling technique, and their relatively moderate expense (partly due to a reduced service to customers).

It may be pointed out that especially as regards the utilization of modern methods of merchandising—as, for example the rational planning of the assortment, the control of the stock, the adoption of the principle of price-lining, the speeding up of the stockturn, etc.—the chain stores have often shown themselves more advanced than department stores.

Moreover, while department stores are or are expected to be "assortment" stores, the chains have followed the practice of picking up and concentrating on the most suitable articles from the point of view of sales volume, rate of stockturn, rate of mark-up, etc., letting the demand for

other, for example, slow stockturn articles, go to the other
forms of retailing.

The development of the unit price store (variety chain)
has likewise represented serious competition for the department store. In America they were already established
before the first world war, but have expanded at an extraordinary rate during the period 1920-1940. During the
same years they have made their appearance and rapidly
developed in Europe.

While the existence of unit price stores translated itself
obligatorily into competition for department stores, one
may say that, as long as these unit price stores confined
themselves, as originally, to carrying only threepenny and
sixpenny (or five and ten-cent) articles, they were not a
serious menace to the department store, since the latter is
organized to handle transactions with a higher average
amount. However, the tendency of the unit price stores to
extend their assortment to higher unit prices, in some
chains up to five shillings (one American dollar) and over,
renders their competition much more serious. This new
technique, with its remarkable efficiency, has not only
increased in the number of its selling outlets, but has started
to embrace a greater variety of those articles which were
formerly mostly purchased in department stores. Finally,
the development of an enterprise like Marks and Spencer
Ltd. in Great Britain has given rise to an entirely new form
of business located halfway between the unit price store
and the department store and which, penetrating deeply
into the assortment of department stores, makes inroads
upon their trade.

The strength of the unit price store derives partly from
the advantages of the chain stores which we have already
listed, amongst which the most important is probably
that arising from large-scale purchasing.

But besides these characteristics, which are common to
all chain stores, the success of the unit price store is due
to other factors, amongst which one must especially note
the selection of the assortment, made so as to carry only
articles which have a high rate of stockturn and which
necessitate only a minimum of sales talk and of selling

service, and the presentation of all the merchandise in the form of open, classified display. The combination of these last two factors has brought a revolutionary simplification of the selling function. The sales talk and the selling work are either eliminated or strongly reduced, while in the department store, in spite of all the division of labour, which centres mainly on non-selling activities, the selling work takes place in about the same traditional manner as in the specialty shop or the ordinary retail shop. Another vital element in the success of the unit price store has been stressed by Törnqvist. It resides in the rudimentary methods used by the retail trade, including the department stores, in the determination of the mark-up and prices. As pointed out by that authority on problems of distribution, one of the causes of the development of the unit price store is the fact that the retail trade, in the determination of its selling prices, is following traditional and irrational methods and does not take into consideration basic factors like the difference in rate of stockturn, and the difference in actual selling service time, which characterize different lines of merchandise[1].

In a country like the United States the development of these new forms of retailing represented by the unit price store and the chain store has been extraordinary. It was not until the beginning of the period under consideration that these new forces began to tell, but when their effect came, it came in full strength. "Fifteen years ago," wrote Filene in 1937, "the department store was considered as a great achievement and the latest and most up-to-date form of retailing. Within a short decade, however, its development has been overshadowed by the tremendous growth of the chain store organizations which have swept the country"[2].

One must further mention, after having reviewed the competition of these new forms of distribution, that those department stores which had a relatively important mail order business have been affected, during this same period,

---

[1] G. Törnqvist: "Detaljhandelns Stordriftsformer", Stockholm 1936, pp. 23-24.

[2] E. Filene: "Next Steps Forward in Retailing", New York 1937, pp. 1-2.

by the decline of the mail order form of retailing. This decline has been due to several causes, among which the following may be mentioned: the greater mobility of the rural clientele, who formed the backbone of the mail order business, on account of the development of motor transportation by private car and bus, allowing it more easily to visit the neighbouring towns and buy in stores; the relative increase of the share of fashion goods in retailing, which are less suitable to the mail order business than are staple goods; and the greater mobility of the market as regards changes in price, style, etc., which causes the catalogue (the main sales promotion medium of mail order business) rapidly to become out-of-date. One may think, on the other hand, that part of these lost mail order sales have returned to department stores in the form of more frequent visits to towns of the rural clientele taking advantage of motor transportation, visits which have, however, been orientated towards the department stores in the smaller towns, rather than towards the department stores of the largest towns.

When recording this decline of the mail order business one must mention an exception, represented by the London department stores, which continue to do a relatively considerable percentage of their sales by mail order.

All the developments, on the whole detrimental to department stores, which we have reviewed so far refer to the competition offered by other forms of retailing.

We must now finally say a few words about a new form of competition, little known in the past, which has revealed itself during the period under consideration and which has prevented retail trade in general, including that of department stores, from getting its former share in the increase of the purchasing power of the public.

This new type of competition consists in an ever-widening struggle for the consumer's money, which takes place not as formerly between the retailers of the same lines of merchandise or even between retailers of different lines, but between retailing itself and entirely different branches of human activity.

This competition is due partly to the fact that the progress of the purchasing power of the public has not kept pace with the development of production or the power of sales promotion. It is also the result of technical progress, of the rise in the standard of living and of the general advance of civilization.

Let us take, for example, the development of the automobile. As long as the purchase of automobiles was confined, as up to 1914, to the higher income classes, it did not markedly affect retail sales. But when, after 1920, the middle or even working classes started to buy cars, it was inevitable that such an orientation of a substantial part of the purchasing power of the public should influence retail sales unfavourably. An American retailer stated as early as 1928: "People spend their money on automobiles, they are less interested in clothing and furniture, and even if they are interested in clothing and furniture, after they have bought an automobile, they have no money with which to buy suits and home furnishings"[3].

Besides automobiles there are radio sets, electric household appliances, beauty parlours and more recently television sets claiming a large share of the consumer's money. It is true that for most of these latter lines department stores have been, by virtue of their very characteristics, in the advantageous situation of being able to carry the corresponding lines or services. But there are besides them, in these lines, a great number of specialized shops, and the share of the department store in the total sales of these lines is probably lower than their share in the total sales of the clothing and home furnishing lines, where part of this money was previously spent.

Furthermore an increasing portion of the income of the public is being diverted to travel, sport, education and leisure activities. Even developments such as the wider diffusion of the telephone, the greater consumption of cigarettes, the multiplication in the number of periodical publications, the progress of insurance, have had their

[3] P. Mazur: "American Prosperity", New York 1928, p. 206.

effect on retail sales by absorbing part of the available purchasing power in new directions.

It is by reason of this evolution that retailing, including department stores, gets a smaller share than previously of the increase in the purchasing power of the public.

During these last decades the competition between department stores became more keen than ever and has even assumed ruthless forms. This was probably unavoidable in a market in which the share of the department stores considered as a whole became relatively smaller and which was therefore being disputed among them with increasing violence[4]. As noted by Emmet, one may say that "individual department stores spend more time watching one another than they do the public"[5]. As we shall see in the following pages, this competition between department store and department store has extended itself to nearly all factors—prices, styles, services, amount of advertising, modernization, etc.—and has rendered trading operations more complex.

One consequence of the developments we have reviewed has had a detrimental effect on retail firms, especially those which, like department stores, feature sales promotion to a large degree. We have already noted in the preceding chapter that during the former periods of department store history there was a considerable amount of unused purchasing power in the hands of the public, and that it was partly by attracting this unused purchasing power that the department store was able to show a tremendous yearly sales increase. From 1920 to 1940 a fundamental change took place from this point of view. While the purchasing power of the population was on the whole higher than that of former days, the "available" purchasing power was lower, because people solicited from so many different sides had developed the habit of spending nearly all they earned—and even more than they earned. The consequence of such a position was that the response of the public to

[4] W. Gabler: "Probleme der amerikanischen Warenhäuser", Zürich 1934, p. 158.
[5] B. Emmet; "Department Stores", Stanford 1930, p. 27.

any sales promotion effort on the part of department stores was less ready than before and brought sales increases of less amplitude, sales increases which were often not profitable when the cost they involved was taken into consideration.

Now this available public purchasing power was not only limited, it was also fixed within fairly narrow boundaries. Thus any artificial increase in purchases brought about by sales promotion was partly offset by the reduction in the purchase of other articles.   In fact, there is, especially for the low income class clientele, a compensatory transfer from one line of articles to another which means that any over-normal increase in the sales of certain lines is gained mainly at the cost of a decrease in the sales of other articles.

When one considers all the factors which we have reviewed in these last pages, one may say that around 1920 the stage was set for a new period of department store history.

Characteristic features of the operation of department stores during the two decades preceding the second world war (1920-1940)

While until the first world war the tradition of the department stores had been, in every country, a tradition of continuous success, they entered after 1920, and especially after 1930, into a new era where they had to forge a new tradition, one of endurance in adversity.

The fact that the department stores were hit by the world depression of 1930-1934 was already in itself a warning that conditions had changed.   In former times department stores had, on the other hand, distinguished themselves by a relatively great staying power in the face of changes in economic conditions.

During the period under consideration, the department stores found themselves in a situation which was somewhat new, in the sense that for the first time in their existence they had entered an era where their sales volumes had ceased to increase in the same way as during the preceding periods.

The time of the great expansion of the department store was over.   The dynamic vigour of the preceding period

seemed spent and the development of that form of distribution brought to a standstill. As a matter of fact, the
department store cycle seems to have reached its culminating
point at the end of the preceding period. It is, for example,
typical that during the period 1923-28, which was one of the
most prosperous in the history of the United States, the
average sales increase of the American department store
was only two per cent. a year[6].

In order to understand the consequences of such a situation one must remember that the great profits made in the
past by department stores were due mostly to the large
yearly sales increases.

As a matter of fact, department stores offer some similarity
to railroads and heavy industrial firms which have a relatively high proportion of inflexible expenses, not directly
affected by an increase or decrease in the volume of business.
The characteristic of such enterprises is that in periods of
expanding sales their profits tend to rise faster than their
sales.

Under these conditions it was natural for the management
of department stores to continue to strive for marked
increases in sales as their main means of maintaining or
recovering the relatively high profits of former days.

In order to achieve this aim they were naturally con-
strained to increase in scope and energy the use of their
main sales promotion instruments, the development of
which we had already noted in the preceding period—
advertising, service to customers and sales events (the
latter tied with the use of articles offered at reduced mark-up).

This was the general tendency of this new era, a trend
already noticeable from the beginning of the period, but
which reached still greater proportions during the depression and thus brought the department stores (with, it
is true, the remainder of the retail trade) into a period
dominated by the use of high pressure sales promotion
methods.

The consequence of this evolution was to increase
continuously the expenses of department stores, mainly

---

[6] Department Store Sales Index of the Federal Reserve Board.

on account of the extension of their services to customers, but also as a result of the growth of their advertising and sales promotion expenses.

Once embarked on this road of increasing service, the department stores were obliged, by dint of the competition between department store and department store, to continue to outbid each other, as it is on the whole easier for the public to ascertain the quality and compare the extent of services between two stores, than to compare the relative quality of their merchandise or even the average level of their prices[7].

It is possible to maintain that we had reached a period when the department stores of the same city competed on service to the public as well as on price or style.

In former days, when the competition of the other forms of distribution and other lines of human activity was not as great, and when the public had a surplus of unused purchasing power, such costly efforts on the part of the department store to secure more business would probably have resulted in a sharp increase in turnover, and the corresponding expenses would have been partly absorbed by the growing sales.

But during the period 1920-1940 these costly efforts, which addressed themselves to a public whose purchasing power was tempted from so many different directions and who, furthermore, frequently already lived above their means, failed to bring any substantial increase in department store sales: the market seemed to have reached saturation point.

As stated by a well-known economist, "All these improvements were adjustments to an era of greater convenience or to an increasing competitive situation. Increased sales—or at least maintained sales—sometimes resulted; increased expenses, however, always resulted"[8].

In the same way high pressure sales promotion, represented by increased advertising of a special type and numerous promotions with mark-up sacrifices, increased expenses

---

[7] H. Smith: "Retail Distribution", London 1937, p. 129.
[8] P. Mazur: "American Prosperity", New York 1928, p. 30.

without bringing on the whole an appreciable increase in sales.

The use of high pressure sales promotion, in particular, has given rise to a new type of advertising whose advisability is very questionable. As noted by Hypps, successful retailing has always been based on distributing goods which the public wants so urgently that the goods will be their own best salesman. It was on this foundation that the success of department stores in the past had been founded. Furthermore, the department stores had understood how to expand the sales of these goods by supporting them through advertising which was mainly considered as a source of information to the public. They were thus in a position to enlarge the sales of articles which would anyhow have found a ready market, but which, assisted by advertising, reached still higher sales. We have already discussed in the last chapter the main reasons which explain, and one may say, legitimize the use, on a considerable scale, of advertising by department stores.

But during these decades one has witnessed, mainly in America, not only an ever-increasing use of this medium but also recourse to a new type of advertising, which we call high pressure advertising. Its mission is not so much to sustain the sales of articles which would anyhow have found a good market as to push artificially the sales of articles towards which the public was indifferent, and in some cases even to impose on the public, by the mere power of suggestion, the purchase of articles that it did not want to buy, and in many cases could not even afford to buy.

The result of such a misuse of advertising has been an artificial stimulation of the sales, but of relatively small degree, usually out of proportion to the outlay of money which it had necessitated.

In the same way an exaggerated use of sales promotion events with sacrifice in mark-up rates (plus later markdowns on over-bought merchandise) and additional sales promotion expenses took place, as if department stores were unaware of the fact that an artificial increase in the sales of a store in one period can always be obtained, but usually at the cost of a decrease of the purchasing power

available to the public in the following period, not to speak
of the corresponding unsettling of the customer's mind as
regards the stability of values.

In fact, the multiplication of sales promotion events and
special offers has been the best evidence that, contrary to
what was the case in the past, the regular prices of department stores did not exercise a great appeal on the public,
and that they were obliged to develop a special price
business in order to attract crowds.

All these abuses are the more important to note, in that
they are mainly found in the department store field. The
other forms of retailing, specialty shops, chain stores, and
unit price stores, have been on the whole free from these
developments, which have, in fact, been mainly weapons of
department stores in the competition within their own ranks.
It is quite possible that their use has allowed a given department store to expand its turnover, at a given time, at
the expense of other department stores. But we know
that in such cases a kind of race, not dissimilar from an
armaments race, takes place. The final result of such con-
tests is that all stores adopt these costly customer attraction
methods, and in the end the average expense level of all
department stores is simply raised.

Even in the cases where these measures of artificial
stimulation have caused a permanent and substantial increase of the sales of the department stores considered as
a whole, they have usually done so only at the cost of
increasing the expenses by a relatively greater proportion
than the increase in sales, thus raising the expense percentage. It is during this period, indeed, that we started to
witness the validity for department stores of an economic
law, familiar in agriculture—the law of diminishing returns.
It has appeared that for the department store too, there is
a point beyond which an increase of sales, brought about in
a saturated market by costly customer services and high
pressure sales promotion methods, does not pay.

But besides this increase in the provision of services to
customers and of the use of high pressure sales promotion,
other factors contributed to make of the department store
an increasingly expensive means of distribution.

One may list among them the increase of the assortment in the various selling departments (as a result of the inventive spirit of industry and commerce); the demand by consumers for greater varieties of goods for selection; and the development of national brands, to which department stores often add their own brands. The department store has remained or become in most countries an "assortment" business where the customer expects to find a wide range. This characteristic represents one of the most positive appeals of this form of business, but translates itself into the obligation of carrying a relatively large amount of stock in relation to the volume of sales. As noted by Emmet, the average department store probably does about two thirds of its business from one third of its stock[9]. Such a situation places the department store in an unfavourable situation, from the point of view of operating expenses, in comparison with the more modern forms of distribution; for the chain stores, the specialty chains and the unit price stores build their assortment by a method of real skimming, selecting only the rapid stockturn articles and simply not carrying the others.

The growing development of fashion, the penetration of the style element into an ever-increasing range of merchandise, making the task of merchandising more difficult, increasing the possibilities of loss from obsolescence and mark-downs and adding to the disposition of consumers to return merchandise, has also contributed to increase the operating expenses of the department store.

The same may be said of the tendency to purchase many items of short life and lower price rather than a smaller number of items of longer life and higher price.

This evolution, in which the department stores have taken a dominating share, has without doubt contributed to remove the danger of the saturation of the market. It has been a powerful weapon of retail trade in general in its endeavour to maintain its share in the fight between various lines of activity for the consumers' money. It can be admitted that without this evolution the sales of retail trade

---

[9] B. Emmet: "Department Stores", Stanford 1930, p. 33.

in general, and of department stores in particular, would be more reduced than they are.

On the other hand, this evolution has helped to transform the assortment of department stores, as the articles dominated or influenced by the style and fashion element are relatively more numerous than previously. As already noted, such a situation has played its part in making department store merchandising much more difficult and costly than before; for a mistake in judgment over style or quantity is more easy to make, with consequences more dangerous than previously.

Furthermore, the fact that nowadays, when a woman buys a hat, she often demands gloves and handbags to match, has obliged department stores to stock a greater number of articles with correlated colours in different departments. This has taken place not only in the clothing group but also in the home furnishing field, with the presentation of highly co-ordinated ensembles based on various colour schemes. Such a development has inevitably increased stocks and mark-down risks, besides making the job of merchandising much more difficult. To quote a single example, the attempt to match the leather colours of shoes and handbags may offer great difficulties, for the simple reason that handbags can be produced in a few weeks whereas shoes may require several months[10].

One must, however, recognize that if this development of the fashion factor has complicated the operation of department stores and increased the cost of operation, it has also contributed to reinforce the position of this form of business in the sense that by their resources and characteristics department stores are perhaps in a better position than most other forms of retailing to study, anticipate, co-ordinate and promote fashions.

Perhaps this question may also be considered from another angle. There is no doubt that the expansion of the unit price stores and of the chains has played its part in reducing the relative share of the department stores in

---

[10] See J. Edward Davidson: "Postwar Merchandising Problems", Journal of Retailing, New York, October 1943.

smallwares, i.e., the articles carried in the ground floor departments. This has displaced the centre of gravity of their trade in the direction of the upper floor departments. These departments entail greater expenses arising from the duration of the transaction, the higher calibre of sales assistant required, and more frequent deliveries; but it is not certain that this particular evolution has been against the interests of the department store.

Continuing our review of the different factors which are responsible for the growing expense rate of department stores, we will recall that we have already mentioned among the services offered to customers the higher standard now required in store fixtures and fittings. As a matter of fact, department stores compete among themselves in modernization as well as in service, price and style; and this serves to increase the expenses.

One must also consider the effect on the operating expenses of department stores of the growth of cities, with their increased rentals, augmented real estate taxes, higher costs of delivery. It may be noted in this connection that, besides the general appreciation of real estate, the very drawing-power of large department stores helps to raise real estate values in the central shopping district. Rentals and real estate values have increased out of proportion to the population, and even out of proportion to buying power.

Finally, higher levels of taxation, decreased working hours, shorter store hours and the pressure of higher wages have borne their share in the increase of the expense percentage of department stores.

Some of these factors, as well as the influence of the factor of growing size, were already at work in the preceding period, and have already been mentioned in the corresponding chapter; but they became more pronounced in the course of the period 1920-1940.

The department store has thus gradually taken a new shape from the point of view of merchandise handled as well as from that of services rendered to the public: from the point of view of physical equipment as well as from that of staff working conditions.

And the operating figures of the new store have become on the whole much less favourable than before. The gross margin (the cost of distribution of the department store) has increased continuously under the influence of these rising expenses. While at the end of the preceding period, in 1914, the average gross margin of department stores was in the neighbourhood of 30 per cent., in 1940 it was tending in countries like France, the United States and Scandinavia to reach 40 per cent.

All the factors which we have just listed are those which have had a direct influence on the rise in the expense percentage of department stores.

Besides these, we may mention some other developments of the period under consideration which, while they have not as directly affected the cost of department store operation, have nevertheless been peculiar to this period. Most of these attempts represent measures taken by department stores to improve their relatively unsatisfactory operating conditions either by means of an increase in their sales, or by an increase in their rate of mark-up or a decrease in their expense percentage.

Among the measures which refer to the increase of the sales is the development of high pressure merchandising, which may be considered as a counterpart to high pressure sales promotion. High pressure merchandising consists of developing, usually in co-operation with manufacturers, articles whose appearance is about the same as the normal articles, but whose price has been appreciably decreased, not by a suppression of useless features or a better adaptation of the articles to their use (as is the case in creative merchandising), but mainly by an abasement of the quality of the article. One may say that in their attempt to increase or simply maintain their sales, department stores have made considerable use of this device, a device whose appropriateness may be strongly questioned. It is true that the general trend of the public towards buying more frequently articles of lower quality instead of buying as previously a more durable article of higher quality, has caused department store men more easily to adopt this practice of high pressure merchandising. But the latter represents nevertheless an exaggeration which has done much harm to the prestige of some department stores. One may think that the transient sales volumes which have been realised by this practice have been more than offset by the bad reputation earned by the stores when the poor quality of the articles has been disclosed in actual wear.

As regards the efforts to increase the mark-up of department stores, they have taken different forms. One must first mention the creation and development of department store chains and of co-operative buying associations to profit from the advantages of mass purchase. There has also been a tendency, especially in the individually operated department store, to trade up (to cater for a clientele of a somewhat higher income class than before). One must also note the efforts to obtain exclusive articles—to carry merchandise that is different from that offered by the competitors, the development of own brands, and the use of creative merchandising[11].

Another indirect consequence of these efforts to maintain and increase the mark-up of department stores has been the increase of the buying and merchandise payroll, as the efforts of department stores to secure an adequate gross margin have often taken the form of an expansion and refinement of the merchandising organization by the presence of more numerous and more specialized buyers, the creation of divisional merchandise managers, and the hiring of specialized executives or assistants.

As regards the former efforts to obtain a more advantageous mark-up by entering into the production and manufacturing field, one may say that these were largely abandoned during the period under consideration, as experience had shown that the most advantageous position for the department store (as probably for any retailer) is one where complete freedom of choice is retained, so that allegiance can be shifted to the best resources and novelties obtained as soon as they appear[12].

---

[11] J. Hirsch: "Der moderne Handel", Tübingen 1925, pp. 242-243.
[12] See Alfred L. Tietz: "Betriebsformen des Grosseinzelhandels. Vier Vorträge über den gegenwärtigen Stand und die Aufgaben des Grosseinzelhandels", Berlin 1931, pp. 27-28.

Some efforts have also been made to decrease the expenses of department stores, or rather to counteract in part the effect of excessive service.

The best-known of these is the development of bargain basements in American department stores where articles are sold with a minimum of service.

Some of these measures may have played their rôle in reducing the decline of the competing power of department stores. But on the whole they have revealed themselves incapable of stemming the continuous increase of the costs of distribution of department stores.

It is, however, only fair to state that in spite of all these shadows the department store has remained to this very day the most important form of retail distribution. Even when it sells at the same or higher prices than some other forms of distribution, it continues to exercise an extraordinary hold on the public.

The great attraction of the department store is explained in part by the elements of customer appeal which it has embodied since its origin and which we have described in earlier chapters. But it seems that there are also other factors, perhaps always partly present in the department store's history, but which have developed in the course of these last decades into powerful elements of added strength.

Thus we have said that with the expansion of the department store one has witnessed the growth of a distinction between the so-called shopping goods (i.e., those which are bought by the customers only after visiting several stores) and the so-called convenience goods, bought near the place where the customers live. And we have noted that the department stores have soon conquered the major part of the shopping goods trade while the so-called neighbourhood stores had to confine themselves to the trade in convenience goods.

But with periodic visits to the department store becoming a regular habit of a growing part of the population, a growing number of convenience goods have been bought in department stores on the occasion of the shopping strolls of customers.

Furthermore, one may note that the multiplication of makes, brands and styles has transformed many convenience goods, notwithstanding their low average price, into shopping goods.

Another powerful element of consumer attraction is represented by the usual location of department stores (even of department stores catering for a popular clientele) in the central shopping district, often in the neighbourhood of specialty shops catering for a high (or at least a medium) class clientele. It seems that the customer belonging to the popular class likes to pass in front of stores of a relatively higher standard before reaching the department store where she shops. As a matter of fact quite often—and it is here that we see the rôle of creative merchandising—the department store will offer to her at reasonable prices, adapted versions of the fine things she has seen in the displays of these higher class specialty shops.

It seems that there are several psychological factors of this kind which play a great rôle and which help to counterbalance the adverse economic and operating factors we have reviewed in these pages.

Such psychological factors are often paramount in the field of retail distribution, and have until recent years maintained the department store as the most representative large-scale retail enterprise.

Development of the department store chains

The expansion of the large department store chains, coupled with a development of methods of organization and operation which are peculiar to this form of enterprise, has also been one of the features of these two decades.

It was probably in Germany that these large chains of department stores first developed and started to utilize new techniques of marketing. The names of big concerns like those of Leonhard Tietz (the present Westdeutsche Kaufhof), Hermann Tietz, Karstadt and Schocken will remain associated with that new and particular form of distribution through department stores directed and operated as the units of a chain.

Similar developments took place in other countries. Thus in Great Britain one may note the development of large chains of department stores like Lewis's Limited, John Lewis Limited and Harrods Limited.

In the United States, whilst the greatest department stores have long been operated as single stores or had only a few branches, mostly of the suburban branch type, one can nevertheless note a parallel movement which has given birth to several large chains of department stores, among which the most important are the Allied Stores, Gimbel Brothers, the May Department Stores, the Federated Department Stores, Macy's, Marshall Field, and the Associated Dry Goods Corporation.

But the greatest impulse towards the development of the department store chain in that country is represented by the entry of the two great mail order houses Sears Roebuck and Montgomery Ward into the retail field, with the creation of two colossal chains of department stores, as well as by the expansion of the Penney Stores.

In France organizations like Paris-France and Nouvelles Galeries control a great number of department stores in various towns of France, while the two greatest Parisian department stores (the Printemps and the Galeries Lafayette) have also a network of branches in the provinces.

Among other examples one may quote the Bijenkorf in Holland, the Innovation in Belgium and the Magazine zum Globus in Switzerland. Indeed these three countries are characterized by the development of the chain of department stores, in contrast to the single department store.

The main cause of the development of these great department store chains, controlling a considerable number of branches, lies in the economy resulting from purchases carried on a greater scale. This question of the economics of the department store chains is discussed at some length in a paragraph of the next chapter.

Organization and control

From the point of view of organization and control, great progress has been made during the period under consideration. Judged by the number and implication of the organizational ideas developed and applied, it ranks as the most memorable in department store history. One may say that the systematic application of the principles of modern management to department store operation started only during these decades.

During the preceding periods the problems of expansion had overshadowed the details of organization. But the result of this situation was that many department stores had grown faster than the ability and techniques of the management. Moreover, the administrative ability and the executive skill of several department store managers were not of the same high order as their commercial sense.

There was thus a definite need for an improvement in the methods of organization and operation. This need has been partially met by the development and application of a series of improvements. Several of these represent organizational ideas borrowed from the field of industrial management, but which have been adapted to the needs of department stores. Reference must be made in this connection to the names of N. Baliol Scott, S. Carlson, W. Kaufmann, J. O. McKinsey, P. Planus, H. Pruppacher and some other management engineers who have made their contributions to this work.

The most important of these improvements which have coalesced into main concepts of modern department store organization, are the following: the introduction of the retail inventory method (or cost and selling system), which makes it possible to obtain at the end of every month and without the obligation of taking a physical inventory the two basic figures represented by the gross margin and the value of the stock; the development and application of a standard classification of the expenses with a dissection in natural and functional divisions; the application of departmental accounting; the introduction of modern methods of merchandise and assortment planning; the use of statistical merchandise control; the development of methods for the control of slow-selling and old merchandise; the introduction of an increased functional and merchandise specialization; the improvement of the grouping of the merchandise lines by a more rational classification and the suppression of confused and heterogeneous assortment of goods; the control of the production and of the expenses of non-selling departments by the selection of units of performance and the determination of unit costs; and the use of market and customer research.

It is also in the course of these years that the loosely linked, almost autonomous selling departments which until then constituted the department store, were connected in a closely knit unified organization.

One may say in general that during these twenty years our insight into the inner workings of large-scale enterprises has been greatly increased and our knowledge in the field of department store organization and management clarified and advanced to a remarkable extent. There are already several stores whose organization and methods conform closely to the modern principles of scientific management. Moreover the groundwork for future investigation has been effectively laid.

Special reference must be made to the resources of modern cost accounting as applied to large-scale retailing. They have made it possible not only better to control costs, but also to discover better means of carrying out the operations. The information supplied by cost accounting, sometimes recorded on a sampling basis, has also enabled the management to explore the possible effects of contemplated changes in policies. This last application is especially important when one considers that the most important business decisions usually refer to the accepting or rejecting of alternatives.

These improvements were not able to turn the tide in the sense that they reinforced, in the firms where they have been employed, the grip of the executives on the operation of the business, rather than brought a revolutionary turn in the situation. But they have nevertheless left their mark. It is, for example, mainly thanks to some of these measures that the percentage of mark-downs in department stores did not increase during this period, and this in spite of the growing importance of the fashion factor in the assortment.

Likewise the increase of the rate of stockturn of department stores in general during this period, in spite of the growing complexity of the assortment, was in relation to these improvements of the tools of management and control.

It is also thanks to the progress made in the field of organization and control that, when the great economic depression of the thirties broke out, several department stores were prepared for the impact.

This growing introduction of modern management methods in department store operation was sponsored by the creation of institutions like the National Retail Dry Goods Association and the Retail Research Association in the United States. As a matter of fact, the former was established as early as 1911 and the latter in 1916; but one may say that their influence started to be really felt in department store operation methods only during the period under consideration (1920-1940). It may be noted, for example, that, while the retail method of inventory was already previously used in a number of American department stores, it was only after 1920 that its application became general, since it was in that year that the United States Treasury recognized the operating results determined on the basis of that method as an acceptable foundation for income tax returns computation.

It is impossible to review the progress made in the application of modern management to the field of distribution without evoking the great influence exercised by Professor Malcolm P. McNair of Harvard University. The names of two other Americans, Daniel Bloomfield, the organizer of the Boston Conferences on Distribution, and Bishop Brown of Pittsburgh University, also deserve mention.

In Europe, reference must be made to the activity of the Retail Distributors' Association Incorporated in Great Britain; and to the International Association of Department Stores, a society for management research in the field of large-scale retailing, established in Paris in 1928 upon the initiative of E. Bernheim, P. Laguionie and R. Sachs, with the assistance of Werner Kaufmann and later H. M. Spitzer[13].

---

[13] H. Pasdermadjian: "Management Research in Retailing", London 1950.

All these developments have given to department stores, in comparison with other lines of retailing, a real lead in the application of scientific principles to the solution of business problems[14].

They may be said to have undertaken the work of scientific research and the application of scientific principles on a larger scale than any other form of distribution, and to have been more hospitable to new organizational ideas than their competitors.

The department store during the second world war

The writing of the history of the department store during the second world war must be left to a time when a better perspective can be obtained. We will confine ourselves to mark here the characteristic features of this period.

In the course of the second world war the department stores, besides paying a direct toll by the destruction of a number of department stores in several European countries, witnessed a complete change in their conditions of operation as compared with the preceding period, with the substitution of a seller's market for the former situation where most efforts were concentrated on the problem of selling and sales development. On account of the great increase of the money in circulation, coupled with a reduction in the production of consumer goods, the emphasis was shifted from sales promotion and merchandising to straight buying: the actual promotion of sales or the selection of the merchandise which would suit the customers ceased to be the great tasks, and the real problem centred rather on the procurement of any merchandise so as to keep the store in operation.

In several European countries and in North America department stores were able to stand the strain of these years and to increase their sales volume, expressed in money. Their expenses also increased, on account of the general rise in prices, and also of the added work of control and record-keeping following the governmental regulations which

---

[14] E. H. Mahler: "Das Warenhaus in der Schweiz", Handbuch der schweizerischen Volkswirtschaft, Bern 1939.

absorbed a good deal of administrative and clerical time, though not incommensurately with the increase of the sales. Furthermore, department stores profited by the sharp reduction in the mark-downs and the decrease of the sales promotion expenses made possible by the existence of a seller's market. Even some rationing measures which brought a forced reduction of the consumption of electricity, delivery, fuel and packing material, had a favourable effect on their expenses.

In consequence department stores like most other lines of business, generally increased their net profits during this period. But this increase in net profit has been on the whole much less marked than during the first world war, because of the incidence of taxation, greater social expenses, and, especially, the much more severe stipulations covering the control of prices and mark-ups, causing in nearly every country a drastic decrease in the gross margin considered as a percentage of sales.

The department store during the years
following the second world war

The years following the second world war have not represented the strong reaction against wartime conditions and the rapid return to buyer's market conditions which were expected. The magnitude of the deferred demand which had piled up during the war years, as well as the economic dislocation left behind by that war, were greater than had been expected.

At the end of the second world war there was in America and in Europe a large volume of unsatisfied demand for all kinds of consumer goods, backed by a great accumulated reserve of purchasing power. That piled-up demand was so great that it has taken from three to five years, according to the country, to satisfy it.

Furthermore the economic and social policies pursued by almost all governments have helped to increase the purchasing power of the population and to liberate (for example by food subsidies and regulated rents) a purchasing power which has found its way into the retail trade.

Thus these years have been characterized by a continuous increase in the sales of all forms of distribution, including the department stores. Since, on the other hand, price control stipulations have imposed on retailers gross profit margins which were appreciably smaller than before the war, this continuous increase in the volume of business has been the major factor enabling the retail trade to operate, like most lines of activity during these years, with satisfactory (or at least apparently satisfactory) results.

Another factor which has enabled the retail trade to operate at a profit during the decade 1940-1950, in spite of much reduced profit margins, is in the conditions of operation characterizing a seller's market, for example: reduction of mark-downs; smaller sales promotion expenses; and smaller selling expenses in a situation where it was often no longer the sales assistant who waited for the customer, but the customer who waited to be served by the sales assistant.

This period was also characterized by a considerable trading up, i.e., meeting a demand on the part of customers for higher qualities, a demand made either in order to make the best use of rationing coupons, or else as a reaction against the poor qualities and synthetic materials of the war period.

All these factors have contributed to hide the fact that in normal times, i.e., in buyer's market conditions, the position of department stores and of the retail trade as a whole is much less strong than appears from their showings during these last ten years. As already stated, during the period 1945-1950 money sales have increased continuously and substantially. In large-scale enterprises like department stores where fixed expenses represent a substantial percentage of the total expenses, such increases in sales represent the most direct road to profits. But these increases in sales have taken place for so long that what was considered at the beginning as an exceptional factor, has tended to become a natural feature of the internal economy of department stores, as of many other enterprises.

It is evident that the return to a more normal market, i.e., to more normal methods of trading, confronts department stores, and indeed many other enterprises, with a great problem of readaptation, the answer to which lies either in an increase of the gross margin rates imposed during these years, or else in increased productivity.

In general the whole 1940-1950 period may be considered, like the 1914-1920 period, as an interruption of the regular sequence of department store evolution. And since a long-range survey like the present one refers mainly to natural tendencies and not to artificial circumstances, it would be misleading to give too much weight to the various episodes and situations which have characterized this period.

In fact, the period may be considered to have had a detrimental psychological effect on department store executives, by making them believe that the favourable results easily attained during these years were the direct outcome of their ability, whereas actually they were mostly the result of external circumstances.

IV

DEPARTMENT STORE ECONOMICS

'Despite the age of the department store as an institution, there is almost no reliable published information on several key questions relative to department store operation. What, for instance, is the best (most efficient and most profitable) size of department store for each of a series of sizes of market? How, and how much, should the significant operation ratios differ for quality-appeal and price-appeal stores of similar size, having similar departments and serving the same or similar cities? What combination of merchandise and service departments ordinarily produces the best results in each of a series of sets of circumstances? There is need for more fundamental research on such questions as these.'—C. Schmalz.

WE have tried to gather in the following pages some information on the economics of department stores, i.e., on the operation of department stores, but considered in its wider aspects. We are moving here in the sphere of what could be called the grand strategy of department store operation. The latter can be directed only in the light of a better knowledge of the major factors which influence department store showings.

We should add that this chapter is mostly based on data referring to the period 1920-1940, since we consider the whole period 1940-1950 as conditioned by special and unrepresentative factors.

The nature of the retail and department store market

Some considerations on the retail market, and especially the market of department stores and on its particularities, is an unavoidable starting point.

For any one who has had the opportunity to watch the retail market and to compare it with, for example, the markets for industrial goods, a number of its distinctive features appear.

First a relatively high degree of mobility. A price change by a single store starts in the great retail centres, in ordinary circumstances, a chain of adjustments of competitor's prices and of reactions. Whereas in the industrial field such

74

reactions may take weeks or even months, in the retail field they are a matter of days, sometimes of hours. This contributes to give a very hectic character to the market and, one may add, to the life of the executives.

There is among many department store executives a feeling that the one who is the first to take an initiative, for example, the first to present new attractive merchandise or to sell an article at a new, reduced price, will be the one who will reap all or most of the advantages, even if his competitors are going to follow suit within a few days.

In a recent and remarkable study, Perry Bliss stressed this factor, showing the importance of timing in department store operation, the constant fear in the mind of the large-scale retailer that his competitor will be the first with some new product or new adaptation of an old product. "If merchandise is offered for sale later than a competitor, the lost sales cannot be made by inducing customers via price reductions". Similarly, the aim of competitive strategy in this field, as represented by special offers, special events, etc., "is primarily to increase his (own) sales at the expense of other stores, and only secondarily to enlarge the total demand . . ."[1].

Another very important factor to take into consideration is that, apart from farming, there is no other line of activity which is as influenced by the weather as retail trade, especially the trade in textile goods. And experience shows that any decrease in sales caused by a series of days of adverse weather is never fully compensated by the reappearance of brighter days. There are even some periods of vital importance for the trade in a number of merchandise lines, especially textiles. A mild or late winter or a cold spring will often spell a very bad season for a department store, whereas, on the contrary, an early winter or spring usually means a substantial increase in sales.

The apparent and the real cost structure of department stores

Another peculiarity of the department store has to be

---

[1] Perry Bliss: "Non-price competition at the department store level", Journal of Marketing, Chicago, April 1953, pp. 363-364.

pointed out here at the beginning of this chapter devoted to the economics of department stores.

Industrial cost accounting distinguishes three major cost components: material, labour and overhead. The study of the cost structure of any line of activity is of great interest because, as stressed by Werner Kaufmann, research and organization pay best where most money is spent or invested.

If we pass now to the field of retailing we may note that this is a field where, as in all commercial enterprises, the accounting methods are different from those of industrial firms. In distribution one starts by subtracting from the sales the cost of the merchandise sold. This gives the gross margin. Then one subtracts from the gross margin the expenses and this gives the net result. The point to stress is that what are considered as expenses in the department store cover only two of the three basic components of industrial cost, namely labour and overhead and not material, i.e., in this case the cost of the merchandise sold.

The important thing to note here is that with a gross margin rate of say 30 per cent. of the net sales, the cost of goods sold represents 70 per cent. of the net sales, and this by any industrial standard would be sufficient to concentrate the efforts of any one entrusted with the task of reducing the expenses on this factor, viz., the materials, which translated into department store terms, means the merchandising aspect.

We must at any rate be aware of the fact that with the accounting practices which department stores have, of necessity, borrowed from commercial accounting, a very important element of loss, the mark-downs, is not included in the total expenses but is already included in the determination of the gross margin.

But the department store trade, especially in its textile groups, is a trade where losses caused by too high operating expenses and the corresponding waste are often much smaller than losses caused by mark-downs (bad purchases, unfavourable weather, general decline in prices).

Thus the chief executives of department stores are in the peculiar situation of executives who, when they review the expense statistics of their firm, never see among these expenses what is often the greatest single item of expenses, namely the mark-downs, as this item is booked elsewhere[2].

This would be sufficient to explain the importance which is attached to the buying or merchandising function in a department store. In reality, if we want to explain the cost and organization structure of a department store by means of a comparison with industry, we may say that the buying or merchandising function plays the rôle of the purchasing division in an industrial firm where the cost of materials would represent 60 to 80 per cent. of the cost price, i.e., exercise a dominating influence on the efficiency of the firm. But more than that. As the buying and merchandising function can influence the result not only by reducing the price at which the store is buying the merchandise, but also by increasing the price at which the store is selling the merchandise (by skilful selection, by creative merchandising), one may say that the buying and merchandising function of a department store does not solely play the rôle of the purchasing manager in an industrial firm, but also, in part, a rôle identical to that of the engineering, research and design functions of a manufacturing firm, which by the excellence of their design can increase the selling price of the goods produced. A similar result can be achieved by the merchandising function by the excellence of its selection, or by its co-operation in the design of the articles.

We think it necessary to stress this point, that the apparent cost structure of the department store does not reveal the whole picture, and may be misleading when considered as a reflection of the total problem of department store operation.

The main factors of retail distribution and their relative use

As is known, the economic theory of production is based

---

[2] One may of course argue that the mark-downs are different from the other expenses in the sense that mark-downs reduce the gross margin, i.e., the cost of distribution, while the expenses proper contribute to increase it. But actually, both elements tend to work alike. A retailer in planning his initial rate of mark-up will mostly take into consideration his average or probable rate of mark-down as well as his expense rate, and will increase his initial mark-up by an allowance calculated to cover this risk.

on the existence of a number of basic agents of production (land, labour, capital) which in practice are expanded into a greater number of factors of production. For example, in industrial economics one deals currently with material, labour, equipment costs and other overheads. One of the main tasks of management resides in the combination of these factors in the most favourable proportions, the more so as there are usually reciprocal relations between these factors.

In transplanting this conception into the field of retail distribution one is inclined to single out the following main factors of distribution (besides the working capital): the location of the store, the space used, the equipment used, the selling personnel, the non-selling personnel, the advertising and display. We have not included in this enumeration the customer services since these mainly represent a combination of the factors equipment used and non-selling personnel. The same remark could of course also be made as regards the factor display, which represents mainly a combination of the factors space, equipment and non-selling personnel; but we have nevertheless maintained display as a separate factor on account of its growing importance, especially in connection with the development of modern methods of selling based on the principle of semi-self-service or self-service selling.

It is arguable that, compared with the smaller retailers, the department store is using to a greater extent the factors of location, equipment, non-selling personnel, advertising and display. On the other hand, it is using to a smaller extent the factor selling personnel. As to the factor space, as distinct from the factor location, the department store usually shows on the ground floor a more intensive utilization of the space available which, in fact, means a relatively smaller use of the factor space. But on the upper selling floors, the situation is often different. One may even note that in some departments, for example, furniture, the department store is often deliberately using the space factor on a pretty lavish scale.

As to the relative use of the various factors of distribution by the most recent forms of distribution, as compared with the department store, one may say that they use the factor equipment on a smaller scale than the department store. In unit price stores the factor advertising tends to disappear completely and the factor selling personnel to be further reduced on account of the use of semi-self-service selling, which results, however, in a greater use of the factor display (perhaps accompanied by an increase in the factor space on account of the method of mass assortment display). The factor selling personnel even fades away almost completely in the stores operated on the self-service principle. But in that case, the use of the factors non-selling personnel and equipment increases and the use of the factor display increases further.

One may also say that this trend in the direction of a greater use of the factors equipment, display, signs and lighting, at the expense of the factor selling personnel is also noticeable in the department store line, especially since the second world war.

In fact we are facing an evolution which we find in all fields of human activity, with a tendency to concentrate the work on equipment, on planning and organization carried out by specialized central units, and a corresponding reduction of the scope of the work of the operator (the worker in industry, the salesman in distribution). In the industrial field, this transfer of work and especially of skill is well-known. In the field of distribution the department store has, since its very inception, followed a similar trend, reducing the scope of salesmanship proper by its use of advertising on a considerable scale as well as by its policy of fixed and marked prices (suppression of bargaining). In the course of these last decades a new step has been made in the same direction by the development of branded articles backed, i.e., pre-sold, by advertising on a national scale, by the use of lighting on a much greater scale and in more refined forms than hitherto, and, more recently, by the introduction of semi-self-service selling, first in the unit price stores and more recently, in an adapted form, in some sections of department stores. All these developments are reducing the scope of salesmanship, especially in the sales of certain lines of goods.

The conception of productivity in retail distribution

The concept of productivity is of course more and more evoked in the industrial field. Already there, i.e., in industry, the measurement of productivity is not an easy job.

This is because productivity is essentially a comparison between the "input" or expenses on the one hand, and "output" or performances on the other hand. And the development of units of measurement is a pretty difficult matter. For the "input", this difficulty comes from the possibilities of interactions and compensatory transfers which may take place between various factors, for example, man-power and equipment. The measurement of the "output" may also raise difficulties, especially in industrial firms which are not process industries but which work on the basis of job orders.

In the field of distribution and especially retail distribution, the same difficulties of measurement exist, but on an even greater scale, especially in the case of the "output".

In measuring the "input" the most apparent unit is probably the salesman-hour, but here too one must take into consideration the possibility of interactions and compensatory transfers between the different factors (selling personnel, non-selling personnel, space, equipment, display).

But the main stumbling block to the study of productivity in retailing is represented by the difficulty—or even impossibility—of determining the output or production. The sales figure is in itself not acceptable in a field where the recording must take place in terms of physical units.

But even the most natural choice, the number of sales transactions, is not wholly satisfactory; for the "production" of retail distribution is not a physical product, but a service, one may even say a series of services, which are of so diverse a nature that is is impossible to sum them up.

There are, besides the sales transactions, such services as delivery and credit. And within the sales transaction there are several components such as the physical transaction proper, the quality of the advice and guidance given during the transaction, the extent of the choice available, the value (relation between quality and price) offered.

Even when considering the production of retailing, i.e., the service extended, from a wider point of view, it is impossible to measure this service properly without bringing into the picture the customers, the inconveniences (or, conversely, facilities) which the customers derive from the service of distribution.

Let us assume that we want to measure the productivity of the distributive trade in a town by making the following relation:

$$\text{productivity} = \frac{\text{number of transactions during the year}}{\text{number of salesman-hours during the year.}}$$

If we now decide to close one store out of two in that town, there is no doubt that, next year, the productivity of retailing measured on this basis will increase sharply on account of a more complete use of the remaining stores.

But for the customers this will mean a greater average distance to the remaining stores and, when in the store, a waste of time on account of queues, waiting to be served, etc.

Thus the increase in the productivity of distribution will be quite theoretical and misleading.

In the same way a department store may have the impression that it is increasing the productivity of the selling staff by reducing, for example, their number and thus shooting up the relation:

$$\frac{\text{number of sales transactions}}{\text{number of salesman-hours}}$$

while, in reality, it will increase only the apparent productivity at the cost of a decrease of the real productivity as judged by the customer.

In reality, questions like the efficiency, the cost and the productivity of distribution are in this field, unlike what obtains in the field of industrial production, closely tied to the services, to the amount of services which are extended by the distributors in any form of distribution and at any given time. This is why it is so arbitrary to state, for example, that distribution was, say, more efficient in a given country in 1946 than at any other time because the gross margin ratio and the expense rates reached at that time a minimum figure.

And in this example we have considered the impact of a reduction in the number of stores on the strength of purely physical factors like the average distance that the customers will have to walk, the waiting time in queues or in the stores. In reality the service represented by distribution is much more subtle than that. Customers choose the stores they patronize not only on the basis of the distance to be walked, but also because of the assortment, the display, the quality of the selling service, the atmosphere, the friendliness. Seen from this angle, the presence in the same area of several stores catering to the needs of the customers in the same line may not represent a waste but a greater real utility for the customers.

One may say that in the field of distribution, there are always two productivities: the first is productivity as viewed or measured by the distributor, the second is productivity as viewed and evaluated by the consumer[3].

The influence of the composition of the trade

We are lacking extensive data on the influence of the composition of the trade on the profitability of department stores.

There are, as is known, different types of department store: those which have a considerable food department, and those which have no food department; those which concentrate on the original department store lines of piece goods, apparel and apparel accessories, and those which have on the contrary given a relatively great development to their home furnishing lines.

It would be of the utmost interest to make comparative studies of the relation which can exist between the composition of the trade and the net results of department stores.

Another approach would consist of analyzing and com-

[3] See on these problems the studies of Reavis Cox and of Wroe Alderson, both published in the Journal of Marketing, Chicago, April 1948 (Number 4, Volume XII).

paring the results given by departmental accounting so as to identify the less profitable lines of merchandise.

The American data, which are the only ones available on departmental results, tend to show that the most profitable merchandise lines were, in the decades preceding the second world war, the men's underwear and accessories department, the ladies' underwear departments (especially corsets, hosiery, but also ladies' and girls' underlinen), nearly all the departments of the ladies' dress accessories group (ribbons, umbrellas, laces, trimmings, handkerchiefs, gloves, jewellery). On the other hand, the least profitable departments were mainly found in the home furnishing group (especially furniture, household appliances, housewares, radio) and in the spare-time requisites group (for example sporting goods, cameras and books)[4].

Not only do these last two groups of departments bring a smaller profit than the others in normal times, they are also the most sensitive to economic depressions. It is interesting to quote here the views of two American authorities, Wess and Schmalz, who regard the home furnishing and furniture groups as decidedly less profitable. Wess, for example, is of the opinion that no department store ought to do more than 20 per cent. of its total sales in the home furnishing and furniture group[5].

European experience also indicates that, on the whole, the textile departments (piece goods, ready-made clothes) are cheaper to operate than the house furnishing departments, as they require less space, involve less transport and necessitate a relatively smaller investment in stocks. On the other hand, competition is usually much more severe in textiles, precisely because new enterprises can be launched with very small financial means, than in home furnishings, where considerable room and an appreciable stock, i.e., a relatively large investment, are necessary to launch a business.

The influence of food departments on the performances of department stores and the question whether the expansion

---

[4] See N.R.D.G.A.: "Departmental Merchandising and Operating Results", New York 1928-1940.

[5] H. Wess: "Profit Principles of Retailing", New York 1931, p. 220.

of these departments is a wise step or not, deserve also to be considered. Such problems ought to be studied on the basis of departmental accounting figures, or better still by determining the contribution of those departments towards the covering of the fixed expenses and the building of the net profit.

Unfortunately in the only country where extensive data are available on the net results of selling departments, namely America, food departments are not developed in department stores.

The influence of the class of trade

Department stores may be roughly divided into stores catering for the popular and middle classes, and stores catering for the middle and higher income classes. While the stores of the first category usually use price as a main appeal, the stores of the second category use quality and service, rather than price, as their main appeal.

As some of the data of American and British origin on department stores make a segregation between these different categories of department stores (which we will respectively call lower income level and higher income level stores) we find it interesting to compare their operating figures[6].

As regards the structure of the sales, the higher income level stores are characterized by a higher percentage of apparel accessories and a smaller percentage of home furnishing than low income level stores, a situation which ought to be rather favourable, as the apparel accessories departments are, as already stated, considered as more profitable than the home furnishing departments.

The initial mark-up of the higher income level stores is greater. The mark-downs are also greater for these stores, but not great enough to offset completely the advantage of mark-up. Thus the gross margin of higher income level stores is greater than that of lower income level stores.

---

[6] See Harvard Bureau of Business Research: "Operating Results of Department Stores and Specialty Stores in 1933", pp. 7-12; and Retail Distributors' Association Incorporated: "Operating Costs of Department Stores", London 1932-1939.

If we turn to the expenses and consider them not as a percentage of sales but in cost per transaction, we see that the cost per transaction is appreciably higher in the higher income level stores. This is due to the smaller number of transactions per salesman and square foot arising from the greater amount of personal attention given to the customer and the smaller number of transactions in the higher income level stores.

However, this greater cost per transaction in the higher income level stores is usually accompanied by an average amount per transaction which is appreciably higher. Thus the expenses of the higher income level stores, expressed not in cost per transaction but as a percentage of sales, are only slightly greater than in the lower income level stores.

The advantages of large-scale enterprises

The main advantages that large-scale enterprises working in any field of human activity (commerce, industry, finance, transport) derive from their mere size, as compared with small-scale enterprises, may be broadly summarized as follows:

1. The possibility of specializing executives, of hiring the best abilities available and of using such specialized minds to full capacity. Closely connected with this factor are two others: firstly, a certain superiority of the large-scale enterprise in the acquisition and the dissemination of specialized knowledge; secondly, the possibility the large-scale enterprise enjoys of picking up the most promising elements from a wider selection basis, and of promoting them to positions where their capacities are best used.

2. The possibility of economies in each of the various resources (money, stock of merchandise, man-power, floor space, material equipment) by pooling these resources in a kind of central mass, necessary to be kept in reserve for ensuring the smooth, uninterrupted, operation of the firm or for exploiting unexpected opportunities.

3. Where the firm combines (as is the case with department stores) large size with a wide range of activities

or lines of products, a large firm derives a decided benefit from the ability to pool the profits of all the lines in a common fund, and to reinvest these resources not evenly but by concentrating them on the development or expansion of the most profitable or promising lines.

4. There is, furthermore, in a large-scale enterprise of the type evoked in 3, a kind of internal insurance which emerges. That is to say, if a line of activity or of product recedes or even dies out, this will often be compensated for by the continuous appearance or expansion of other lines.

5. The possibility of using the principle of division of labour in its most complete form, so as to specialize operatives and increase their ability or use their special aptitudes to a fuller extent. This higher degree of division of labour results in the creation of a number of jobs of great repetitiveness and uniform character, jobs especially amenable to job study and rationalization.

6. The possibility of using, on account of the scale of the operation and of the factor described under 5, specialized, mechanical, labour-saving equipment, especially in production, and material handling. Furthermore, in several lines of production, material handling and, especially, power-generating equipment, the unit investment and unit operation cost decreases with the increase of the capacity of the equipment, which represents a further incentive to large-scale operation.

7. The possibility of buying on better terms, by virtue of the size of their orders. Furthermore, the possibility of savings in operating expenses, resulting from the larger average size of their commercial transactions and shipments.

8. The possibility, with top executives, of delegating not only specialized tasks or supervisory duties, but even part of their work of administration proper, ensuring thus that the firm will have one or several brains free for creative thinking.

9. The possibility of engaging in research work and experiments, as this nearly always means a long term

outlay of money with returns which cannot be predicted with certainty. More generally, the application of scientific fact-finding is more likely to be found in an enterprise of some size than in a small enterprise.

10. The possibility of systematizing operation and control by developing standards of performance and standard methods of operation for repetitive or recurrent activities. This is tied up with a certain amount of research (see 9) and a minimum scope of operation.

It must be stated that in the case of the department store it is perhaps especially the factors listed under 1, 2, 3 and 4 which are important. As regards factors 5 and 6, one may say that department stores derive smaller benefits from them than do industrial enterprises. For example the wide variety of the goods found in a department store sets pretty narrow limits to the possibilities of mechanization which, even in a field like material handling, are connected with a certain degree of standardization.

As to factor 7, one may note that the possibility of buying on better terms on account of the size of the orders refers mainly to the chain of department stores or to the very large single store. As to the savings in operating expenses on account of the size of the orders, they apply, in the case of department stores, to the transactions on the buying side, not to the sales transactions.

As to factors 8, 9 and 10, the extent of their action depends on the degree to which modern conceptions of management are accepted by the top managers of a firm, rather than on the field of activity of the enterprise.

The influence of the size factor within the retail and department store field

The influence of the size factor on, the operation of department stores may be now considered within the retail field and from two different standpoints: firstly from the point of view of the unit size of department stores in comparison with the unit size of other forms of distribution, and secondly from the point of view of the influence of the size factor within the department store field itself.

From the first of these points of view one may note that no other form of distribution has a unit size which is as large as that of the department store, as even the greatest chain stores are working by means of branches, each of which is considerably smaller than the average department store. The department store is and remains the most important and most concentrated single unit of retail enterprise.

This greater unit size of the department store confers on it distinct advantages from the standpoint of division of labour, the use of specialized auxiliary departments, and the performance of the non-selling operations on a larger scale with corresponding savings. For example, in accounting, training, advertising, display and delivery, the department store is able, on account of its greater unit size, to effect these operations better (by the presence of qualified specialists) and more economically than other retailers. It is true that the chains and unit price stores are able to concentrate some of these activities in their central administration and thus to profit from the same advantage—with, however, the drawback of a less intimate contact between these central organs and the selling units, on account of the distance separating them.

For example, at a time when personnel management and training activities are assuming such importance, the greater unit size and the centralized character of the operation of the department store place the latter at a distinct advantage.

The larger unit size of the department store brings several other advantages. It creates prestige, permits a more effective layout of the departments, striking displays of merchandise, and makes possible (at least theoretically) an economic use of customer services and publicity.

Against these advantages the department store suffers the inconvenience of a greater rigidity in operation, which is a consequence of its greater unit size and of the existence of a considerable administrative machinery. As noted by Hypps, department stores find it more difficult, on account of their size, to make adjustments. The handicap of store investments and the risks involved in accepting new ideas complicate their competitive problems when viewed in relation to other forms of retailing, including chains and unit price stores. The lower store investments and the great flexibility of these businesses permit them to adopt newer methods without the risk of great loss if the venture proves of little merit.

The question of the influence of the size factor may be treated from another point of view in considering the effect of the size factor within the department store field itself.

The material at our disposal for examining this question comes from Great Britain and America, as these are the only countries in which considerable data on the operating figures of department stores, grouped by size, are available.

The British figures show us that, except for the department stores catering for a relatively high income level clientele, where there is no correlation between size and profits, the profitability of department stores increases with an increase of the size of the store. The majority of the expenses (functional divisions: 'administration', occupancy', 'buying' and 'selling') decline, when considered as a percentage of sales, with the growing size of the store[7]. The only exceptions are represented by the 'publicity' expenses (or rather the advertising part of the publicity expenses) and the 'delivery' expenses, which tend to increase with a growing size of the store, as the greater stores must draw their clientele from a wider territory and serve their customers in a wider area.

But apart from these exceptions the expense percentage decreases with increase of size; and this is logical enough, as one could expect that the larger the size of a department store, the greater the possibilities of saving by a fuller utilization of personnel and premises, and the greater the opportunities of ensuring the economies of large-scale operation.

The American figures show, on the other hand, that the larger the size of a U.S. department store, the larger the

---

[7] See Retail Distributors' Association: "Operating Costs of Department Stores for the year ending January 31st, 1938", London 1939.

total expenses (in percentage of sales)[8]. It is true that even in American stores there are a few functional divisions of expenses like 'administrative and general' and 'display' which tend to decline with growing size, and others like 'buying and merchandising' and 'direct and general selling' which seem unaffected by the factor; but the sharp increase of the expenses of the functional divisions 'occupancy', 'advertising' and 'delivery' determine the net increases in total expenses.

This irrational situation is a further illustration of the fact that American department stores, in their strenuous fight for volume and exaggerations of customer service, drifted in the period between the two world wars into a position where the advantages of the greater economy inherent in operation on a large scale were nullified.

Up to about 1930-1933 the largest American stores were able to compensate for this greater expense by means of a greater gross margin and a greater rapidity of stockturn; but in the following years their advantage in gross margin had not been great enough to offset their larger expenses, and the department stores of middle size have, on the whole, been more profitable than the largest stores.

The general conclusions which may be drawn from all these data appear to be as follows:

With an increase in the size of the department store the expenses of the functional divisions 'advertising' and 'delivery' increase (when considered as a percentage of sales), while the expenses of the functional divisions 'administrative and general' and 'display' decrease.

As regards the expenses of the functional divisions 'occupancy', 'buying and merchandising', 'direct and general selling', they tend to decrease with growing size of the store in countries like Great Britain where the operation of department stores has been maintained within reasonable standards. But they remain unaffected by size, or tend even to increase with size, in countries like America (and probably also France) where the department store had reached a very

---

[8] See Harvard Bureau of Business Research: "Operating Results of Department Stores and Specialty Stores in 1938".

advanced stage of evolution with the appearance of several symptoms of economic degeneracy.

It might also be that some of the American and Parisian department stores have exceeded the maximum single size most suitable for economic or efficient operation.

In fact, it is possible that there exists for department stores, as for any form of enterprise, a maximum size above which the increase of the scale of operation does not pay. As stated by H. Smith: "Under modern conditions the most efficient size of an enterprise is mainly determined by a balance between the economics of large-scale production, which are essentially the advantages gained by splitting processes of production into specialized operations, and the growing cost and difficulty of effectively co-ordinating all these processes as their number increases. In any given state of technical knowledge and stage of development of the art of scientific management, it is certain that, from the point of view of producing (or distributing) as cheaply as possible, an ideal size for the firm in any industry will exist. If the firm is smaller, technical inefficiency will outweigh the ease and cheapness of management, while, if it is larger, then almost certainly it will be top-heavy with expenses of management"[9].

A given department store may thus reach a unit size which is too big for efficient management. But this of course may happen only in the case of very large stores located in the largest cities of the world.

In other cities, a large department store, the largest department store in the city, is usually at a distinct advantage over the other stores, first on account of the larger size of its departments (i.e., of the assortment) and secondly because the suppliers, especially those who have exclusive goods, are likely to approach him first.

Furthermore, when a store has a selling area let us say 20 per cent. larger than a direct competitor, it has very often administrative and fixed overhead expenses not much larger than those of its competitor, and is thus able to absorb them on a larger turnover. This comparison, however, holds

---

[9] H. Smith: "Retail Distribution", London 1937, p. 121.

true only for small differences in size. If the difference in size is appreciable the inevitable difference in organizational set-up destroys the validity of this argument.

At the other end of the scale there must also be a minimum size for efficiency, under which a department store cannot take full advantage of the potentialities this form of business comprehends, both from the point of view of economic purchase, of minimum size of the departments and of efficient operation by the presence of specialized personnel and equipment. In studying the American and British data on department stores, grouped by size, one has the impression that this minimum size for efficiency was around a turnover of £100,000 per year before the second world war. When taking into consideration the figure of yearly average sales per employee, this would mean that this minimum size for efficient operation was in the neighbourhood of 100 employees.

However, this question of the minimum size for a department store is also influenced by the size of the town in which it is located. Thus Elizabeth A. Burnham has found in her statistical investigation of the data provided by 426 American department stores, that there is apparently a minimum sales level, within each city size, below which a department store finds it difficult to operate effectively[10].

The administrative machinery of department stores and its cost

There is a widespread belief that one of the causes of the decreasing profits of department stores lies in the fact that, with the refinement of their organization and management techniques and the growth of their size, the administrative expenses have increased in such a proportion as to represent a steadily increasing burden.

It is worth while to examine objectively the evidence at our disposal on this question, so as to see if that belief is in keeping with the facts.

It is true that the administrative machinery, mainly represented by specialized executives and employees and

---

[10] See E. Burnham: "The department store in its community", Harvard Business Review, Summer 1940.

additional control systems, increases with the growth of the size of the store and the progress of management. But one must keep in mind that in a large store these administrative expenses can be distributed over a larger sales volume. One must also take into consideration the fact that the large department store offers wider opportunity for efficient division of labour, for using labour-saving accounting and office machines and devices, and for employing, in general, the economies of large-scale production in administrative work.

We have at our disposal the detailed expenses of department stores classified in groups according to their size for only two countries, Great Britain and the United States; and, as already pointed out, the expenses of the functional divisions 'administration' or 'administrative and general' decrease, when expressed as a percentage of sales, with a growing size of the store, in both countries[11]. We have also seen that in Great Britain it is not only the expenses of the division 'administration', but the total expenses of department stores, which decline with a growing size of the store.

It is true that in the United States the total expense percentage shows an opposite trend and increases, as already reported, as the stores grow in size. But in analyzing the various expense items of American department stores one finds that the larger stores are those which have the smallest administrative expenses (functional division 'administrative and general') expressed as a percentage of sales, and that their greater total expense percentage is due to other factors (mainly greater 'occupancy', 'publicity', and 'delivery' expenses).

This does not mean that there are not great possibilities of saving on the administrative side of the operation of department stores, and this is especially the case in the larger stores where the administrative expenses, if they are relatively smaller, are greater in absolute figures and offer thus

---

[11] See Retail Distributors' Association: "Operating Costs of Department Stores for the year ending January 31st, 1938", London 1939, pp. 21 and 51; and Harvard Bureau of Business Research: "Operating Expenses of Department Stores and Departmentized Specialty Stores", 1938, p. 13.

greater opportunities for economies. Furthermore, the comparison of the data of American and British origin over a number of years shows that in the course of the period 1928-1938 the average administrative expenses of department stores of the various size groups have tended to rise. There is thus an unquestionable need for a continuation of the efforts made to increase the economy and efficiency of the administrative machinery of department stores, but with a clear view of the possible scope of this question, which is too frequently commented upon without knowledge of the facts.

Division of labour in department stores

From the viewpoint of organization the economics of the department store centre mainly on the resources, the advantages and the limitations of the application of the principle of the division of labour.

We have already seen that this principle is at the very origin of the creation of this form of distribution. It is a form of organization where the auxiliary functions are performed in specialized non-selling departments, allowing the buyer or department head to concentrate on the main commercial functions, i.e., the buying and selling of goods. Furthermore, this centralization of the non-selling activities in auxiliary departments makes it possible to work on a large scale, to adapt the staff of the non-selling departments more exactly to the fluctuations in activity, and to use, as regards methods and equipment, all the resources of standardization applied to repetitive jobs.

One must, however, be aware of the fact that the possibilities open to department stores in this last direction are more limited than for example in the case of large-scale industrial enterprises. This is due to the fact that a department store, even when it reaches a very large size, is composed of widely different but relatively small selling and non-selling departments. One will find in the latter jobs which are characterized by great repetitiveness; but those jobs are rarely performed on a very large scale, in the sense that there are a great number of people doing the same job. Moreover, in distribution (contrary to most industry) the repetition of the jobs is rarely absolute, i.e., the jobs may be similar but not identical, on account of the existence of one or several variable factors (typical example: a wrapper who is wrapping boxes of similar shape but of various sizes).

But this is after all only one of the possibilities afforded by division of labour. There are many others open to the department store, and from which it can derive its strength provided it has the will to exploit them.

We have already said that one of the main advantages of the department store lies in the possibility it affords of centralizing the auxiliary, non-selling, activities, in the specialized departments. The same applies to certain parts of the work of planning, conception and research. But one must be aware of the fact that these specialized agencies can be really useful only if the line executives (in that case the buyers/department heads) have the vision and the courage to use the services of these specialized agencies. Often this is not the case. And one may say that one of the problems of department store organization lies in the conflict between two opposite forces. There is, on the one hand, the legitimate desire to place the buyer/department head in a position where he feels that he has a certain responsibility; and this can be achieved only by giving him a certain liberty of action, a certain autonomy. There is, on the other hand, the presence in a department store of these central or centralized agencies which embody the resources of the principle of the division of labour and represent one of the strengths of this form of business. If the buyers/department heads are free to use or not to use these organs, according to their will, they will often not use them at all, and a large store will remain, from this point of view, a mere collection of small enterprises.

Difference in operating conditions between the department stores located in the largest and smaller towns

In investigating the difference in operating conditions between the stores located in the largest and the smaller towns on the basis of the data available on American and British stores, certain observations are possible.

The gross margin is higher in the stores located in the largest cities. This is possibly due to the fact that such stores being on the average larger, they are able to secure more favourable buying prices on account of their larger purchases. It may also be that the greater merchandising skill and resources at the disposal of the larger stores make it possible for them to carry a greater proportion of non-comparable merchandise whose price is not dominated by competition.

As regards the expense percentage, we find it to be higher in the stores located in the largest cities. Indeed, American data show that the expenses of department stores tend to vary in direct proportion with the population of the towns in which they are located. This is logical enough: for example, occupancy expenses are appreciably higher in the largest cities. The same applies to the delivery expenses and also to the publicity, since the department stores located in great towns have to use advertising to a greater extent in order to attract customers in face of a stronger competition than that which faces the department stores located in smaller towns.

The only items of expense where the department stores located in the largest towns are at a relative advantage are the buying expenses (probably because they are usually located nearer to the resources), and the selling expenses, on account of their fuller utilization of the personnel (greater number of transactions per sales assistant) and probably also because of a higher degree of division of labour.

But taken as a whole, the expense percentage of department stores located in the largest cities is greater than that of the department stores of the smaller towns.

As to the question of the net profit, it obviously comes down to whether the greater expenses of department stores of the largest cities are more than compensated by their greater gross margin.

The British figures would tend to show that, whilst until 1932 the average net profit (in percentage of sales) of the provincial stores was higher than that of the London stores, the contrary proved the case from 1933 up to the second

world war. In the course of these last 12 years new factors
seem to have again given provincial stores the advantage,
especially those catering for a popular clientele.

In America the evolution had been in an opposite direction. Until a few years before the second world war the net
profit percentage tended to grow with an increase in the
size of stores, but during the last years preceding the second
world war stores of moderate size, i.e., stores mainly located in smaller towns, tended to show better rates of earning
than the largest stores.

Among the reasons which have been given in explanation
of this, the following may be noted. It is possible that stores
located in smaller towns with a population from 25,000 to
100,000 inhabitants have an opportunity to create institu-
tional reputations at a lower cost than stores in large cities.
When well managed, they can frequently dominate their
local market to a greater degree than the stores in larger
cities. They are often able to draw considerable trade from
outlying areas without feeling obliged to provide free
delivery service to those areas. They enjoy the lower wage
rates reflecting the lower cost of living in the smaller cities.
The increased traffic congestion in large cities, the increased use of automobiles in rural areas, and the increased
knowledge of branded merchandise among consumers have
likewise favoured the stores located in the smaller towns.
Another explanation of the greater profitability of these
stores in recent years may lie in the lines of merchandise
handled and the type of supplementary business carried on.
These stores of moderate size have a tendency to concentrate
their efforts on what may be called straight dry goods,
apparel and closely related merchandise, with only minor
excursions into other, and often less profitable, merchandise
groups[12].

However, Elizabeth Burnham's very complete investigation into the influence of the size of the population of the
towns in which department stores are located, on their
operating expenses, while confirming this trend, has raised

---

[12] See Harvard Bureau of Business Research: "Operating Results of
Department Stores and Specialty Stores in 1937", p. 24.

two qualifications. Firstly, it is noted that department stores
located in towns with a population smaller than 25,000
inhabitants find it difficult to obtain sales of sufficient
volume to ensure efficient operation; secondly, by pointing
out that in the smaller towns and in the towns of middle
size it is usually the department stores with the largest sales
which have the most favourable expense percentages and
the greatest profit opportunities[13].

The influence of the rate of stockturn on the operating results

In its report on the operation of department stores in
the year 1928, the Harvard Bureau of Business Research
has grouped operating results according to the rate of stockturn (counted on the basis of the beginning and ending
inventories, and not the monthly inventories)[14].

These figures, which are relatively old and which cover
only American department stores, are nevertheless interesting to reproduce, as they represent the type of investigation
which throws some light on the economics of department
store operation.

	(all figures in percentage of sales, except the rate of stockturn)		
	Department stores with a rate of stockturn of		
	less than 3 times	3—3.9 times	4 times and over
Average rate of stockturn ...	2.7	3.4	4.8
Mark-downs	7.4	6.5	6.2
Gross margin	33.3	32.6	33.6
Total expenses	32.6	31.8	31.2
Net profit	0.7	0.8	2.4

These data show, first, that whilst the rate of mark-downs
not unnaturally decreases as the rate of stockturn increases,
nevertheless the gross margin does not seem to be markedly
affected by differences in rate of stockturn.

The result of a faster stockturn seems to be primarily
reflected in a lower percentage of total expenses rather

[13] See E. Burnham: "The Department store in its community",
Harvard Business Review, Summer 1940.

[14] Harvard Bureau of Business Research: "Operating Expenses of
Department Stores and Departmentized Specialty Stores in 1928",
pp. 15-16.

than in a greater gross margin. The more detailed data reproduced in the publication quoted above show that it is especially the expense percentages of the natural division 'interest' and 'salaries', and of the functional divisions 'administrative and general' and 'direct and general selling', which are reduced by a higher stockturn, whilst the expenses of the functional divisions 'publicity' and 'buying and merchandising', on the other hand, have a tendency to rise with a higher rate of stockturn, though not enough to prevent the total expenses from declining.

The final result is that the highest net profit is shown by the highest stockturn group and the lowest net profit by the lowest stockturn group.

The rise of the rate of stockturn concurrently with the 'publicity' expenses has been recorded by some authors, like J. Hirsch[15]. This relation was, however, more pronounced in former days than in the years which preceded the second world war.

Besides this American investigation we have also British data on the same subject[16]. In the latter study the analysis is first made along the same lines as above, that is to say by grouping together those stores which have certain rates of stockturn. The results are about the same as in the American study, and show that the gross margin variations do not seem to be caused by the rate of stockturn, while, on the other hand, the total expenses show a definite downward trend as the rate of stockturn increases.

But the British investigation uses also a second approach, where the influence of changes in the rate of stockturn on the other operating figures is investigated. These investigations show that an increase in the rate of stockturn, for a single store, generally brings an increase of the gross margin (probably by a reduction of the mark-downs or a change in the composition of the trade), a decrease of the total expenses and an increase in net result.

---

[15] J. Hirsch: "Das amerikanische Wirtschaftswunder", Berlin 1926, p. 61.

[16] Retail Distributors' Association: "Operating Costs of Department Stores for the year ending January 31st, 1934", pp. 10-15.

The influence of the rate of mark-downs on the operating results

The Harvard report already quoted shows, by a suitable dissection of the results, the influence of the rate of mark-down on the operating figures of American department stores[17].

	(in percentage of sales) Department stores with a rate of mark-down of		
	less than 5 per cent.	5—7.4 per cent.	7.5 per cent. and over
Average mark-down rate ...	3.8	6.4	8.3
Gross margin	32.7	33.6	33.9
Total expenses	31.5	32.1	32.5
Net profit	1.2	1.5	1.4

Whilst gross margin and total expenses increase as the percentage of mark-down increases, the net profit is greatest for the middle group.

An explanation of this result resides perhaps in the fact that whilst the group with the greatest mark-down percentage reflects a corresponding weakness in the merchandising and stock control, the group with the smallest mark-downs does not, in many cases, imply merchandising skill, but an abnormal composition of the trade with too great a weight on staple merchandise or too crude operating methods with an exaggerated rigidity of mark-up.

A more comprehensive investigation, of British origin, on the relation between mark-downs and the profitability of department stores has brought the following, more differentiated, observations[18].

In the department store catering for a popular income class clientele the most successful stores have been found to be those with the highest initial mark-up and also the highest mark-downs, that is to say the stores which practise the policy of marking their merchandise at relatively high prices for a very short period and then quickly lowering

[17] Harvard Bureau of Business Research: "Operating Results of Department Stores and Departmentized Specialty Stores in 1928", p. 17.
[18] Retail Distributors' Association: "Operating Costs of Department Stores for the year ending January 31st, 1933", London 1934, pp. 8, 18 and 19.

them to clear a large proportion of their stock at reduced but still profitable prices. This trading policy secures them a relatively high maintained mark-up, in spite of relatively high mark-downs, and gives them also a more rapid stock-turn. The less successful stores of this class of trade show, on the contrary, relatively lower maintained mark-up in spite of the fact that they show virtually no mark-downs.

The analysis of mark-downs in the stores catering for a high level clientele reveals a quite contrary state of affairs. In this category the stores which show the most favourable net results are those which have the smallest rate of mark-downs.

The conclusion is thus suggested that the large mark-downs of the most unsuccessful stores in the higher class of trade result from faulty merchandising, whereas those of the most successful stores in the lower class of trade indicate a deliberate policy of showing goods for a short time at relatively high prices and subsequently disposing of remaining stocks at considerably reduced but still profitable prices. These impressions are confirmed by the rate of stockturn. The large mark-downs of the most successful stores in the lower class of trade can hardly be due to faulty buying, for their rate of stockturn is exceptionally high. At the other extreme the heavy mark-downs of the least successful stores in the high class trade are clearly due to faulty merchandising as their rate of stockturn is particularly low.

The influence of sales increases and decreases on the operating results

We have already pointed out the fact that many of the expenses of a department store being of a relatively fixed character, any increase or decrease of the sales has a marked effect on the net result.

The Harvard figures referring to the American department stores for 1928 have also been grouped according to rate of sales increase or decrease during the year[19].

---

[19] Harvard Bureau of Business Research: "Operating Results of Department Stores and Departmentized Specialty Stores in 1928", pp. 12-14.

		Department stores showing a		
		Sales decrease over 2.5 per cent.	Sales increase or decrease less than 2.5 per cent.	Sales increase over 2.5 per cent.
Gross margin	...	32.6	33.5	33.4
Total expenses	...	33.0	31.8	30.7
Net result	....	0.4	1.7	2.7
Rate of stockturn	...	3.5	3.9	4.1

(in percentage of sales, except rate of stockturn)

The consequence of a sales increase is, on account of the fixed character of many expenses, a reduction of the total expense ratio which results in a better net result. On the other hand, a decrease of sales brings, for the same reason, an increase of the total expense ratio, with an unfavourable effect on the net result.

In considering the detailed expense figures which are included in the original publication, one finds that stores with increasing sales volume have a relative advantage (i.e., smaller expense percentages), as regards the natural divisions, in 'salaries', 'rentals', 'advertising' and 'interest'. When considering the functional division of expenses, we find that the expense percentages are lower for the stores with increasing sales volume for all the functional divisions, with the exception of the functional divisions 'direct and general selling' and 'delivery'. The conclusion which may be drawn from these data is that among the expenses of department stores those covered by the functional divisions 'direct and general selling' and 'delivery' are those which, in times of rising sales, have the most proportional character, i.e., have a tendency to rise as rapidly or nearly as rapidly as the sales.

In the case of a declining volume of sales we find similar fluctuations, but opposite in direction, the expense percentages of the natural divisions 'salaries', 'rentals', 'advertising' and 'interest', as well as all the functional divisions (with the exception of 'direct and general selling' and 'delivery'), increasing concurrently with a decrease of the sales volume.

As regards the rate of stockturn, we find, as expected, that the stock has a tendency to turn faster with increasing sales and more slowly with reduced sales.

The influence of retail price rises and falls on the operating results

The influence of retail price rises and falls on the operating results of department stores is the most potent which can be imagined. In fact, when considering the history of department stores, one sees that the most spectacular increases in profits from one year to the next have been caused by a sharp increase of the general retail price level, while on the contrary the most marked fall in profit has been due to a violent decline of the retail price level.

This relation between price level fluctuations and profits is a consequence of the following fact: it costs as much for a retail store to sell a pair of stockings at, say, $0.80 as it did to sell it last year at $1.00, but the gross margin out of which all expenses must be taken will be 20 per cent. less.

The influence of an increase or decrease in the number of transactions on the operating results

An increase or decrease in the number of transactions has a direct effect on the expenses of a department store, an increase in the number of transactions bringing an increase in the expenses, whilst a decrease in the number of transactions brings (or ought to bring) a decrease in the expenses. As a matter of fact, the expenses of a department store are more influenced by the fluctuations of the number of transactions than by the fluctuations of sales, as the latter are often caused by a fluctuation of the retail price level, or of the average amount per transaction, which are both without great direct influence on the expenses.

Fixed expenses in department stores

We have just stated that an increase or decrease in the number of transactions has a greater influence on the expenses of a department store than an increase or decrease in sales. But neither an increase nor a decrease in the number of transactions brings a directly proportional variation of the expenses, because one of the main economic features of the department store is that a large part of its expenses are fixed.

Such expenses as rentals, real estate costs (including property taxes), interest on funded debt, depreciation on buildings and fixtures, insurance, are fixed, i.e., do not show fluctuations with changes in the volume of business.

The same applies, if not to quite the same degree, to such items as the salaries of executives and key employees, and lighting, heating and cleaning expenses.

As to the items of expense represented by the wages of the selling personnel and of the employees and workers of the non-selling departments (especially the following: receiving, marking, delivery, accounts payable, sales dissecting, accounts receivable), these are semi-fixed or semi-variable, in the sense that they fluctuate with changes in volume of business, but relatively less than these changes.

On the other hand there are items of expenditure, as on supplies and repairs (the latter mostly for psychological reasons), which are truly variable.

The behaviour of sales promotion expenses depends mostly on the policy of the store. In many cases where an increase in volume is brought about by external factors (for example general business conditions) these expenses will tend to remain fixed. On the other hand, in the case of declining sales these sales promotion expenses can be variable when the management decides to budget them according to a fixed percentage of sales, but they can also remain fixed or even increase if the management decides to counteract the decline in sales by maintaining or even increasing its sales promotion expenses in absolute amount.

In fact the experience of department store operation reveals that in a full-size department store the fixed expenses represent from 65 to 75 per cent. of the total expenses, at least when considering variations in the volume of business within a certain range (increase or decrease). In the case of an increase in the volume this is the range within which the additional volume of business can be mastered with the available personnel, equipment and premises, or with very small additions to them.

It is this high proportion of fixed expenses which explains the sharp fall in, or even the elimination of, the net profit in periods of declining sales volume, and, on the other hand, the relatively great increase in net profit brought about by a relatively small increase in the sales volume.

However, when the fluctuations in volume exceed a certain range, the proportion given above for the fixed expenses ceases to be true, because the wages of the selling staff, and the expenses of a number of non-selling departments, especially receiving, marking, delivery, accounts payable and accounts receivable, increase markedly and rapidly, while the depreciation expenses as well as other expenses also tend to rise.

But even in that wider context of greater changes in volume the fixed expenses still represent from 25 to 35 per cent. of the total expenses.

Relation between the net results and the operating figures

The following comparison is taken, as are the preceding ones, from the 1928 report of the Harvard Bureau of Business Research[20].

The available operating figures of American department stores are classified according to the rate of net profit or net loss as follows:

(in percentage of net sales, except rate of stockturn)

	Net loss	Department stores showing a		
		Net profit less than 2 per cent.	Net profit 2—3.9 per cent.	Net profit 4 per cent. and over
Gross margin	32.0	33.0	34.1	34.1
Total expenses ...	34.2	31.8	31.1	29.0
Net result	—2.2	1.2	3.0	5.1
Rate of stockturn ...	3.5	3.7	4.2	4.2

While the percentage of gross margin is greater for the stores with higher profit, the principal difference is in total expense ratio. The stores making the best profit were primarily those with the lowest total expense ratio. In considering the detailed expense figures reproduced in the publication quoted, one notes that the expense rates were noticeably smaller, in the case of the most successful stores, for the natural expense divisions 'salaries', 'rentals', 'advertising', and 'interest', and in the functional divisions 'ad-

---

[20] Harvard Bureau of Business Research: "Operating Results of Department Stores and Departmentized Specialty Stores in 1928", pp. 19-20.

ministrative and general', 'occupancy', 'direct and general selling', and especially 'publicity', whilst there was no marked difference in the expense ratios of the functional divisions 'buying and merchandising' and 'delivery' between the stores of various degrees of profitability. Once again the significance of the stockturn as an index of profitability is confirmed, stores showing net losses commonly turn their stocks more slowly than do the stores showing a net profit.

The occupancy expenses of department stores

Nearly all expense items controlled by the store management function have markedly increased during the last decades before the second world war. This applies also to the occupancy expenses, on account of the growing requirements of the department store line as regards the background upon which the business is conducted, of the rise in real estate values, and sometimes also of expensive real estate entanglements.

But it is worthwhile to record, when measuring the relative position of department stores, that for the rentals or real estate costs, which represent the main item of the occupancy expenses, the data available show that in this respect the department store continues to maintain its natural advantage over its competitors by virtue of its extensive use of the cheaper upper floors. Thus the real estate cost of department stores represented on the average about four per cent. of sales, whilst in the specialty shop located in the central shopping section of great towns, rentals frequently represented between six and ten per cent. of sales and reached still higher figures in the specialty chains. Even the unit price stores, which show smaller expense figures than the department stores for nearly every division of expenses, are not at an advantage as regards their rental or real estate expenses, for these are usually of much the same order as those of department stores.

As already stated, this advantage of department stores lies in their use of the cheaper upper floors as selling premises, while the other forms of retailing are mainly using the expensive street floor.

It is worth while to note in this connection that the development of the escalator is likely to reinforce still further the position of the department store, ensuring an even better use by the clientele of those cheaper upper floors which play such an important rôle in the reduction of the average occupancy expenses of this form of retailing. The effects of this technical development, when fully exploited, may reveal themselves as more far-reaching than is commonly imagined.

Economics of department store chains

We have noted the appearance and expansion of the department store chains, those enterprises controlling and operating a number of department stores located in different towns.

Perhaps it is only in the course of the last decades that all the implications of this form of business have started to be understood, and its advantages utilized in the development of the technique of central buying and central merchandising. Those chains of department stores which have really adopted these methods (and they are still a minority) have obtained the reduced prices resulting from mass purchases and the elimination of the wholesaler. In doing this they have of course been obliged themselves to assume the function of the wholesaler; but—and this is perhaps the real advantage of the chains of department stores—it has soon emerged that the central buying and central merchandising organization of a chain is in a position to assume the function of the wholesaler at a smaller expense than a wholesale firm. These advantages of the chain of department stores, when it does a job of central buying and central merchandising, over the wholesaler, have been well summarized by Törnqvist[21] The variety of different articles carried by the chain which has to deal only with its branches and which can therefore to a certain degree impose the assortment, is of necessity smaller than that of the assortment of a wholesaler, who has to consider the wishes of a greater number of different retailers, and this smaller

---

[21] G. Törnqvist: "Detaljhandelns Stordriftsformer", Stockholm 1936, pp. 28-30.

assortment represents smaller distribution expenses and at the same time a greater concentration of purchases, i.e., more advantageous purchase prices. The closer contact between the chain and the branches than between the wholesaler and the retailer translates itself into central stocks of a smaller size, into more rapid and complete information on customer demand (quantities, varieties, styles, etc.) and also into smaller distribution expenses (the chain treating the branches as units of the firm, whilst the wholesaler has to consider the retailers as customers, which involves expenses of direct or indirect publicity, granting of unreasonable claims, loss of time due to politeness, conventionalities, necessity to visit the retailers one by one instead of gathering the representatives of all the branches to present them the assortment jointly, etc.). One must also take into consideration the elimination of credit extension and collection costs between integrated units.

It has been estimated that because of the savings listed above, the cost of distribution of a chain of department stores (or a chain store) which effectively practises central buying and central merchandising represents, for its wholesale function, only about one half of the cost of distribution of an ordinary wholesale firm.

Such a chain of department stores is usually able to show a gross margin which is, other things being equal, higher than that of an individually operated department store. Its expenses are also higher, as a chain of department stores performs to a greater degree wholesaling functions, the cost of which is included in its gross margin. But, as already stated, because of the greater efficiency of the chain of department stores over the wholesaler, this increase in the expenses is not as great as that of the gross margin.

Further, besides the decrease in expense brought about by the integration of the functions of retailing and wholesaling realized in the chain of department stores with central buying and central merchandising, there is also an increase of efficiency caused by the more effective co-ordination between the production and distribution activities, and by the possibility of utilizing the abilities of the specialists within the organization to better advantage.

Thus the chain of department stores represents a more profitable form of operation than the individually operated department store, on account of its superior buying power and lower expenses.

In practice, this advantage has not been gained by all chains of department stores but only by those which have really exploited the possibilities afforded by that form of enterprise; which are operated along the principle of central buying and central merchandising; and in which the central organization does not confine its activity simply to receiving and retransmitting the orders of the branches, but co-operates actively in the planning and determination of these orders so as to achieve the necessary degree of standardization in the assortment, and to ensure the discounts which result from large single orders[22].

But there are still a number of chains of department stores which are not operated along these lines and are thus not in a position to make full use of these natural advantages. In several cases the cost of distribution of these chains of department stores is not less than that of the individually operated stores, but is on the contrary more, because these firms, instead of adopting frankly the principle of central buying and central merchandising, have created a central buying organization while maintaining the former buying organization in the branches, so that they have to bear the expenses of two buying systems instead of one[23].

Finally a few words must also be said on a factor which, at the time of the creation of the chain of department stores, was supposed to represent an appreciable advantage but which has revealed itself inoperative. Taking into consideration the fact that fashion took from six months to a year to penetrate from the capital or the fashion centres to the provincial towns, some of the early promoters of the chains counted on that lag of time to solve the problem of

---

[22] Alfred L. Tietz: "Betriebsformen des Grosseinzelhandels. Vier Vorträge über den gegenwärtigen Stand und die Aufgaben des Grosseinzelhandels", Berlin 1931, p. 27.
[23] Harvard Bureau of Business Research: "Operating Expenses of Department Stores and Departmentized Specialty Stores in 1928", p. 21.

mark-downs: the goods which would be out of fashion in the main store would be shipped to the provincial branches. Experience has shown that the whole system fell down, partly on account of the speed with which fashion travels nowadays, partly for other reasons. As a matter of fact when a chain of department stores has a main store in the capital and branches in the provinces, movements of merchandise between the branches, if they take place at all, are more likely to take place from the branches in the direction of the main store, which being located in a great city has better opportunity to organize on a large scale the special sales necessary to get rid of the remnants.

Department stores and the various forms of integration

As a conclusion to this chapter we find it advisable to consider the department stores from the point of view of the kinds and degrees of integration which they represent. As a large-scale enterprise is in fact always an example of integration under one form or another, a review of that type of enterprise from that angle will offer a convenient way of summarizing its economic characteristics.

According to the definitions developed by Professor D. H. Robertson and Professor P. Sargant Florence, we will make a distinction between horizontal, lateral, vertical and diagonal integration.

Horizontal integration considered not as the diversification of the line of products but as the mere increase of the scale of operation in a given field, i.e., producing or distributing the same product or line of products, but on a larger scale, finds (as already noted) little application in the single department store. But it is encountered in the chain of department stores which can reach volume in many lines of products on account of the duplication of the same selling department in several branches.

On the other hand, lateral integration, in the sense of product diversification, i.e., the production or distribution of different lines of merchandise by the same enterprise, is the very essence of the department store in all its forms (single stores or chains of department stores). As is known, it is this gathering of a great number of different lines of merchandise under the same roof which has represented the great element of customer attraction and sales promotion of the department store. The department store has been one of the illustrations of the fact that in the commercial field the appeal of a full line (in this case of complementary lines) makes the whole more powerful than the mere sum of its parts.

It is also this aggregation of different lines of merchandise in department stores which alone has made possible the creation of retail stores of a large unit size at a time when chain stores were still in their infancy, and allowed some retail firms, the department stores, to profit by many of the advantages of the large-scale enterprise [24]. New lines, i.e., new selling departments, were readily added with the feeling that any such addition would contribute to spread the existing overhead expenses on a wider basis.

In their search for expansion the creators of the first department stores, which were nearly always single stores catering for a given community, have soon found that beyond a certain point intensive development, in the sense of great and rapid sales increases in the lines already carried, was impossible, and they turned to extensive development by means of lateral integration, i.e., by means of a greater diversification of the lines of goods distributed.

However, with time, with the development of the chain stores, we have witnessed the creation of a different type of large-scale enterprise, the firms which do not need to use the resources of lateral integration, in the sense of a wide range of different lines of goods, in order to attain a great size. These firms have grown without using lateral integration, by multiplying the number of their branches without widening their assortment. In doing so, they may have forsaken the advantages of lateral integration but they have reaped other advantages, such as a greater concentration of buying power and a greater specialization of their personnel.

As to vertical integration, one may note that hardly any department store confines itself to the retail level, but

[24] E. J. B. Lloyd: "The department store as a method of retailing", The Liverpool Trade Review, January 1953.

undertakes, partly or wholly, some activities which are usually connected with the function of the wholesaler. This integration of the retail and of the wholesale levels is most pronounced in the large chains of department stores and we have pointed out in the preceding paragraph, devoted to the chains of department stores, how such large-scale enterprises engaged in the field of distribution, and which integrate the retail and wholesale levels, may eliminate or simplify a number of commercial acts.

There are also some cases where vertical integration extends over three levels: retailing, wholesaling, and manufacturing, with a department store controlling manufacturing interests. There are still examples of this nowadays, mainly in the men's wear, women's wear and furniture fields. But these vertical integrations on three levels are relatively rare in the department store field and one may say that the trend during these last decades has been in the opposite direction, i.e., several department stores have liquidated their interests in the manufacturing field, as they have found that such an extension of their activity to manufacturing was a source of weakness rather than of strength, except perhaps in times of great difficulties of supply, as in war periods.

Such extensions to the manufacturing sector usually spread the energies and the mental resources of the management over too wide a field. Furthermore manufacturing in such "captive" manufacturing units, working only or mostly for a single retail firm, cannot always attain the scale where economic production is possible. In fact the two preceding factors are connected. Either the manufacturing unit produces only or mainly for the department store which controls it, and, in so doing, cannot reach the scale of economic production; or the manufacturing unit produces on a scale where economic production is possible. But in this latter case a major part of the production has to be sold to outsiders, with the consequent creation of new problems of merchandising and marketing which distract the top managers of the department store from their main mission.

There is another factor perhaps more peculiar to such fields as clothing and home furnishing where the elements design, fashion and style play a dominant rôle, and which counteracts vertical integration up to the manufacturing level. As is known, in industry this vertical integration upwards often takes the following form. An industrial enterprise will acquire or create a subsidiary firm which will supply the main enterprise with a raw material or a part entering into the manufacture or the assembling of its own product. But this subsidiary firm will be selected or designed so as to have a capacity of production which represents, say, 60 per cent. of the consumption of the mother firm in times of great activity, the remainder (i.e., the other 40 per cent) being still bought from outside, independent, suppliers. This enables the mother firm to reduce and even to stop its purchases from outside sources in times of business depression and to concentrate its purchases on its own subsidiary, which will thus continue to work at full capacity even in times of depression. The burden of maintaining an excess capacity of production in times of reduced economic activity is thus thrown on the outsiders. As is known, this set-up is found, and this policy followed, by several industrial firms.

But in the department store line such strategy is hardly possible on account of the predominance of the factors design, fashion and style. Thus, even (indeed especially) in times of depression, a department store which would have planned a scheme and a policy similar to those we have just evoked in the case of a manufacturing firm, would not be in a position to reserve its purchases entirely or even predominantly to its own manufacturing subsidiary. In a field as versatile and changeable as the one of fashion goods, and in a market as competitive as the retail market, one is obliged to buy always from the best supplier, and in such lines it is rarely the same firm which is the best for a long time.

In fact, the main drawback of the ownership by department stores of their own manufacturing resources has been found to be the reduction it causes in the liberty of choice of the buyers or department heads as to the selection of their sources of supply, and this has shown itself to be a major handicap in a field like clothing and house furnishing where competition is so active and success often so short-lived.

Thus the production activities of department stores are usually limited to minor fields, such as some alteration and repair workrooms, or such auxiliary activities connected with the food trade as baking, confectionery-making, tea-blending, or coffee-roasting.

But it is interesting to point out that while the present tendency of large-scale retail enterprises, including department stores, is towards the abandoning of the manufacturing field, there are, in the case of some very large chains of department stores and of large chains of variety stores, a tendency towards vertical integration into the manufacturing field, but under a new form. These large-scale retailers do not manufacture, they buy their goods from independent suppliers; but they nevertheless penetrate indirectly into the field of manufacturing through the influence which they exercise by means of co-operation between their own experts and the manufacturers. This co-operation takes the form of advice and recommendations in matters of design, creation, product simplification, industrial engineering (planning, tooling, job simplification) and cost accounting.

While vertical integration was always viewed until now in the form of acceding to and gaining financial control of a new level in order to reduce costs or to increase profits, there is here a new form of vertical integration, where greater efficiency by means of better synchronization between various levels is attained by the extension of free co-operation in the form of specialized knowledge without any actual penetration by means of financial control.

Finally diagonal integration, in the sense of the provision within the enterprise itself of auxiliary services to the main functions, finds numerous applications in department stores. The existence of so many different lines of merchandise serves to create a demand for auxiliary services, which reaches sufficient strength and continuity to be centralized and efficiently performed in the firm's own ancillary services—as for example an advertising department (instead of the services of an outside advertising agency), display department, delivery department, maintenance department, statistical machines department, research department, etc. In some cases the firm will even have its own power plant and its own printing plant.

As to the influence of the economic conditions on integration in the department store field, one may note that times of depression, like the 1930's, have induced the department store to retreat along the road of vertical integration, by liquidating some of its manufacturing interests. These are times when the possession of a manufacturing unit is often a handicap, as similar goods can be bought at smaller cost from outside manufacturers selling at no profit or even at loss. On the other hand, such times of depression work differently on lateral integration, which may progress on account of the efforts of department stores to maintain their shrinking volume of sales by entering into new lines of trade. Thus on the Continent several department stores have really entered into the food line in the 1930's. Conversely, a time of pronounced boom and seller's market somewhat temporarily revives the interest of department stores in vertical integration and in the manufacturing units which they still own, and reduces their interest in further lateral integration.

V

THE ECONOMIC AND SOCIAL INFLUENCE OF THE DEPARTMENT STORE

'But the Bazaar is a factory: it has taken unto itself the several phases of the economic circuit, and now contains them all. And it is also a factory of smiles and visions, of faces and dreams of life, surrounding people with the commodities for which they live, holding out to them the goals for which they struggle. What factory is geared so deep and direct with what people want and what they are becoming? Measured by space or measured by money, it is the greatest emporium in the world: it is a world . . .'
—C. Wright Mills.

IF the department store is in itself the result of changed material conditions, it has not failed to influence in its turn the economic and social evolution of our age, by its existence and by the movements it has initiated.

It is the influence of the department store in the economic and social field that it is proposed to consider here in a rapid survey.

The department store's coverage

Under the term department store's coverage we understand the degree to which department stores cover the retail market, i.e., in fact that proportion that the total sales of all the department stores represent in the total retail sales.

The data available on this question which refer to the 1930's are as follows:

	Turnover of department stores as a percentage of the total retail trade of the country
Denmark	3 per cent[1]*
France	5 ,, ,, [2]
Germany	4·5 ,, ,, [3]
Great Britain	7·5 ,, ,, [4]
Spain	1 ,, ,, [3]
Sweden	3 ,, ,, [5]
Switzerland	4 ,, ,, [6]
U.S.A.	9 ,, ,, [7]

* See footnotes on opposite page.

As one can see, the sales of department stores represented a relatively small percentage of the total turnover of the retail trade of the various countries.

However, one must take into consideration the fact that food lines, which account for nearly 50 per cent. of the total retail trade turnover, are only slightly represented in department stores.

Actually a study of the coverage of the department store ought to be limited to the clothing and home furnishing lines, which represent about 80 per cent. of department store sales.

It must also be borne in mind that department stores are a form of retailing not found in the country, the villages or very small towns. If we therefore determine its coverage by confining ourselves to towns above a certain size and to the clothing and home furnishing trade, we find that the coverage of department stores is then around 30 per cent. in America and between 10 and 20 per cent. in Western Europe.

In some specific lines, such as piece goods and women's and children's clothes, the coverage of the department stores is even greater.

The conclusion is, nevertheless, that the degree of concentration reached in retailing is smaller than in industry or in finance, as in this field the traditional forms of distribution, i.e., the small shopkeepers, still account for more

[1] J. Hirsch: "Skandinaviske Detailhandels-Normtal", Copenhagen 1938, p. 93.

[2] Forschungsstelle für den Handel: "Der Einzelhandel in Frankreich", Berlin 1930, p. 117.

[3] International Chamber of Commerce: "Europe—United States. Distribution Problems", Paris 1931, p. 93.

[4] H. Smith: "Retail Distribution", London 1937, pp. 49-51.

[5] J. Hirsch: "Standard Figures of Scandinavian Distribution", Copenhagen 1938, p. 21.

[6] Eidg. Preisbildungskommission, Bern 1933.

[7] The American statistics for 1928 and 1929 gave the share of department stores in the retail trade of the United States as 15-16 per cent, but these percentages are exaggerated, as they include, beside department stores, general merchandise stores and variety chains. The American Business Census of 1933 gives, more correctly, the share of department stores as 9 per cent.

than half the total retail sales. Retailing is, as a matter of fact, one of the fields where monopolistic or quasi-monopolistic situations are unknown.

It has been stated that in the long run, in every line of business, competition determines which type of business is to survive. It appears that in the field of distribution, unlike some lines of production, there is place for both large and small units. As recently stressed by John Ramage: "The justification for active competition between the large number of retail shops of differing type and size is that it enables the diverse needs of consumers to be met . . . Shops are not alike in size, appearance, in the services they offer or in the goods they expose for sale because of the immense variety and diversity in the needs and tastes of consumers. Rival shops do not merely compete: they complement each other"[8].

The department store and industry

The department store has played a not negligible part in the development of modern industry, in those branches of industry devoted to the manufacture of consumption goods. It has assisted in awakening needs without which a whole series of productive processes would perhaps not have got beyond the small craftsman stage.

Certain branches of industry are, in fact, indebted to the department store for their present development. This is particularly the case with the clothing industry. The vast majority of women's garments were, until the middle of the 19th century, made at home either by the customer or by a dressmaker. As for men's clothing, people who were comfortably off ordered their clothes from their tailor, while the others bought theirs at a second-hand clothes shop. The great development of making and selling ready-made clothing for women and men was, for the most part, the result of the activities of the department stores, which started and popularised ready-made clothing[9]. Thus, in

[8] The Fortnightly Review of the Drapers' Chamber of Trade, London 28th August 1953.

[9] F. Ambrière: "La vie secrète des grands magasins", Paris 1938, p. 22.

Paris, from 1860 to 1890 (that is to say, during the period of expansion of the department stores), the number of people earning their living from the clothing industry was almost quadrupled[10].

In the same way, in the field of the furniture industries, the department stores have placed all sorts of articles within reach of a large public.

Thanks to their contacts abroad, their experience and their documentation, department stores have also, in several countries, played a considerable part in developing the production of goods for which those countries were, until then, dependent on foreign manufactures. For example in France, it was they who assisted in the creation, in the second half of the 19th century, of the carpet industry, making goods which France previously imported from England[11]; in collaboration with French manufacturers, they replaced the toys from Nuremberg; they participated in the development of the French knitwear industry to break the virtual monopoly which Berlin and Chemnitz had held for decades[12].

In Germany it was thanks to the action of the department stores that certain industries, for example those of household utensils and furniture, were able to switch their manufactures into new directions and thus to reach and satisfy the needs of the great masses[13].

It must also be noted how, by their methods of sales promotion, department stores have ensured to certain branches of industry, particularly to the textile industry, a much wider market than that which these industries would have had to accept, had they merely depended on more traditional forms of retail trade to provide them with facilities for disposing of their products. As will be emphasised in a later chapter, different branches of activity are today engaged in a veritable struggle to ensure for them-

---

[10] G. Michel: "Le commerce en grands magasins", Revue des Deux Mondes, 1st January 1892, p. 151.

[11] G. Michel: p. 147.

[12] G. d'Avenel: "Les Grands Magasins", Revue des Deux Mondes, Paris 15th July 1894, p. 346.

[13] J. Hirsch: "Der moderne Handel", Tübingen 1925, pp. 224-225.

selves as large a portion as possible of the purchasing power of the public. There is indeed no doubt that by their methods of publicity, presentation and sales, department stores have prevented the portion accruing to the textile industry from being reduced by exaggerated proportions. Industrialists have been well aware of this influence. Thus, it was that, when in 1936-1938 the French department stores found themselves facing difficulties because of the charges to which they were subjected, the French textile industry was disturbed and declared that a diminution of the sales of the department stores would not be entirely compensated for by any increase in the sales of other forms of distribution, and would eventually result in a reduction in the French consumption of textiles.

From this point of view one may compare the department store to a locomotive pulling a train composed of wagons, each of which represents a line of industry: textiles, dress accessories, home furnishings, etc. If the locomotive slows down the whole train follows the change in speed.

One may also say that the department store has succeeded in re-establishing a balance between production and distribution which had been destroyed. For the erstwhile situation, in which the small trader did business with a craftsman or with a small undertaking, the industrial revolution substituted at the beginning a new situation, in which the small retailer found himself up against more powerful industrial or wholesaling enterprises. The department store has established once more the equilibrium. There appeared with it a form of distribution which was in a position to deal on equal terms with industrial undertakings.

But, with time, we have witnessed a new evolution. The large-scale manufacturer is, thanks to his elaborate marketing organization, in a position to serve not only the large-scale retailers, but also (and one may even say, especially) the small-scale retailers.

On the other hand, the small-scale manufacturer, who often experiences difficulties in reaching the retail market, especially the small retailers, finds in the large-scale retailers, with their merchandising organizations, the best channels for marketing his products. The development of national

brands and resale price maintenance by important manufacturers has made this tendency even more noticeable: the
large-scale manufacturer counts on selling to the great
number of small retailers whom he is in a position to reach
and serve, as much as to the large-scale retailers.

Department stores have made a contribution to the
consumer goods industry by putting at its disposal their
creative energy, their foresight and their strength in
organizing and distributing.   Very often their buyers
have been a driving force behind the manufacturers.

"Retail trade is in the habit of ordering in small amounts
not long before delivery. In addition, and often because of
local circumstances rather than as a consequence of adapting
itself to the desires of consumers, it demands very varied
models for the same article. The result is that the manufacturer cannot adopt a regular rhythm of manufacture and
is obliged to produce small amounts of different types of
goods, conditions which prevent him from obtaining his
minimum cost price"[14].

The department store, on the contrary, by its methods of
merchandising, by its buying and assortment plans, by the
orders it passes in advance in bulk, has facilitated the task
of the industrialist and permitted him to prepare his manufacturing programme and to organize his production in the
most economical way and with longer runs.

It is the influence of the large department stores and
of the chain of department stores (besides, of course,
that of chain stores and unit price chains) which has been
especially felt in this direction. These large-scale merchandising organizations have often used their massive purchasing power to offer manufacturers contracts for continuous operations or orders which can be made complementary
to their other operations or orders. When one knows the
importance of capacity utilization and of fixed costs to
modern industry, one understands the opportunities which
exist in this direction. Some spectacular price reductions
of articles which used to belong to a definite price level,

[14] P. Laguionie: "Organisation de la distribution au détail", Paris
1938, p. 7.

are due to this use by large-scale retailers of the characteristics of modern industrial economics. The chain of department stores is in a specially favourable position to exercise bulk bargaining power, and to reduce manufacturing costs by the facilitation of long runs.

On the other hand, for an industry concerned with the production of consumer goods and above all the production of fashion goods, one of the most exacting of its activities consists in anticipating future tendencies of the market. There too, the orders from department stores are a valuable indication, for it is on these orders that the industry bases its forecasts of market trends—not the trends of the advance guard, but the trends which will be followed by the greater part of the market.

Finally, the special sales events of the department stores very often permit the industrialist to dispose of stocks still on hand, or to provide work for his establishment during periods of lessened activity.

Representing an integration of wholesale and retail undertakings, employing the speediest methods of observation and exploitation, the department store measures the real needs of the consumer, stimulates and orientates the producer. As the head of a large Belgian commercial enterprise has remarked: "Between, on the one hand, the old conception of trade as the prolongation of production, and on the other hand, distribution in the modern sense which, reversing the rôles, proceeds from a study of consumption in order to condition production, there is the difference which distinguishes empiricism from method"[15].

Sir George Schuster most appropriately defined the rôle of department stores in this connection when he said that the task of these undertakings consisted of "interpreting and orientating the demand of consumer markets and transmitting this demand to manufacturing industry in the form of orders conceived and handled in such a way as to encourage production under the most economical conditions".

---

[15] E. Bernheim: "La distribution des marchandises", Brussels, 1937, p. 6.

The influence of the department store on markets

When trying to discover the influence of department stores on markets, as well as on the purchasing and consuming habits of the public, it must first of all be said that, by its working methods, not only its fixed and marked prices, but also by its principles of free entrance and by its advertising, the department store has reduced the differences in price which previously existed for identical or similar articles.

It has produced a sort of levelling of prices which has been to the public advantage. One might even go so far as to claim that it is the department store which has given to the clothing and furnishing trades the character of a real market. In order that the law of supply and demand should work freely, in order that for a given article prices should be established which, if not identical, are at least in proximity, it is necessary that certain conditions of publicity be fulfilled, that certain possibilities for making comparisons be assured to the public. There is no doubt that the shopping habits which the public have been able to contract, thanks to the principle of unrestricted entrance, as well as that kind of permanent quotation represented by the advertising insertions of the department stores, have played an essential rôle in this evolution, and that numerous abuses which could have lasted only if the public had not been completely informed, have been eliminated.

For the rest, it is to the department stores that we owe the tendency of feminine customers not to make any purchase until they have made comparisons in price and quality between competing houses. But the department stores have also supplied the needs of quite a different sort of clientele, those who desire to buy without devoting too much time to the choice of their supplier. As Colson remarked, "the good or bad reputation of an undertaking, of which the name is in keeping with the extent of its operations, guides the purchaser who has not the time to make these comparisons for himself"[16].

It is also relevant to remark that the department stores have helped to give, by the rapid succession of goods they

offer and by the quickened tempo which they have effected
in fashions, a more dynamic character to the market. They
have led the public to visit the stores at shorter intervals,
to make their purchases more often, instead of allowing
their needs to accumulate and their purchases to be made on
widely-spaced visits. In this way, they have their share of
responsibility for the greater mobility of social custom
which characterizes our time.

As far as relations between the customer and firm are
concerned, there is no doubt that the department store,
compared with older forms of retail trade, has brought
with it a certain 'depersonalization' of the sales transaction.
The relations between customer and sales assistant, or
between customer and firm, have a much less personal
character in the department store than in the specialty
shop or the small undertaking.

This depersonalization of the sales transaction has its
unfavourable aspects; but it also presents some advantages.
It often guarantees a more equal treatment of all customers.
This has often been seen during the difficult years of the
second world war. During this period of shortage of
goods, the customer often had the feeling that she was
treated less highhandedly and was less at the mercy of the
whims of the salesman in the department store than in the
small retail undertaking[17].

The social effects of the department store

In considering the social effects of the department store,
one is inclined to attach the greatest importance to the
contributions which they have made to the transformation
in the way of life of the greatest strata of the population, a
transformation which will remain the one great social fact
of these last 100 years.

"The principal cause of the success of the department
stores," declared G. Michel as early as the end of the last

---

[16] C. Colson: "Cours d'économie politique", Paris 1903, IV, p. 236.
[17] See on this subject the very significant results obtained from an
inquiry based on the population of Belgium in 1946 and carried out
by the Belgian Institute of Economic and Social Information. Published in "Opinion Publique et Marchés", Brussels, April-June 1946,
pp. 14-19.

century, "is that their founders understood that, to a new social system whose needs and habits were changing, it was necessary to offer, on the best possible terms, means of satisfying tastes for elegance and comfort unknown to previous generations"[18].

By using new principles of merchandising and of commercial policy, the department stores placed within reach of the public a whole series of articles which had, until then, been reserved for those classes that were most well-off. They have assisted in spreading the sense of comfort and the taste for luxury. To use the expression of Emile Zola, "they have democratised luxury".

G. Michel demonstrated this rôle of the department stores by examples in 1892. "Twenty-five years ago," he wrote, "a pair of skin gloves of good quality cost six francs, today the same pair of the same quality is sold for four francs, and it is made in a whole series of lower qualities, of which the price goes as low as 1.50 francs. It is the same in all the special lines without exception".

The department stores have thus lowered the price of a number of articles, by turning to good account new productive processes. They have 'treated' articles in such a way as to give them a particular character. Finally, by their sales promotion activities they have created vastly augmented public needs and won over the customers to new consumption and to the use of articles about which they previously knew nothing.

This action has resulted in a reduction in the difference between the modes of existence, and even the appearance and outlook, of the different classes of the population.

"Before the war of 1914," wrote P. MacOrlan, "I lived on the banks of the Seine, in front of the Javel quarter. Every morning very early I was in the habit of taking my little fox terrier for a walk. It was just at the time when the factory whistles and sirens rent the melancholy heavens with their joyless appeal. I met on my way workers of every age, young and old, who were hurrying spiritlessly

---

[18] G. Michel: "Le commerce en grands magasins", Revue des Deux Mondes, Paris 1st January 1892, p. 138.

towards the groaning ill-tempered signal. All the women were marked by life, a hard, unsatisfying and even pointless life. With their hair tight, their shoulders covered with a shawl of indeterminate colour, the rest of their clothes completely devoid of personality, they were the sort that Steinlein used so often to draw sympathetically and lovingly. When I came back from the war, everything in the morning picture of my district had changed. Pretty girls, neat and stylish girls with short hair, many of them with their heads covered by a little 'cloche', their stockings straight, were on their way to the same factory, the same office. It seemed to me that something had changed, at least in appearance. It is certain that the department stores are at the root of this transformation. In my opinion, their greatest claim to recognition lies in the fact that they have succeeded in giving a particular character to things which, until then, seemed to be impervious to all style"[19].

Ambrière quotes for his part a great industrialist, a character in a modern comedy who cried: "All is lost! My employees are dressed like I am". And in fact today the head of a business and his secretaries look as though they have the same tailor, the typist rivals in elegance the boss's wife[20]. Ambrière further declares that at the root of this outward levelling-off there is the activity of the department stores.

We will confine ourselves to noting that one of the main characteristics of our time resides in the fact that some fashions, some needs, some events which in former days reached or affected only a small minority or an elite, today touch a much wider circle.

But the department store has not only reduced the existing difference between the modes of life of the various classes of the population. It has also approximated the modes of existence of the various parts of the country, diminished the contrast between the capital and the provinces. Madame Marcelle Tinayre declared that the transformation that

---

[19] P. MacOrlan: "Le Printemps", Paris 1930, pp. 88-90.
[20] F. Ambrière: "La vie secrète des grands magasins", Paris 1938, pp. 224-225.

occurred in provincial life was above all due to the automobile and the department store catalogues[21].

Some approve of this influence, saying that the department store has thus contributed towards the broadening of
the horizon of part of the public, towards the elimination
of barriers between the different sectors of the population.
Others reproach the department store with having had its
share in the responsibility for spreading this contagious
influence from the big cities to the small towns, from the
small towns to the country, with the result that part of the
population has contracted the habit of living above its
means.

This last influence has been brought to light by Emile
Zola, who remarked that the first department stores, by
their processes of selling and of presentation, have not
only awakened new desires, but have represented a strong
temptation for the public. "It is the woman for whom the
competing department stores contended among themselves,
the woman whom they continually caught in the snare of
their special offers, after having rendered her dazed and
stupefied in front of their displays. They were a huge
temptation to which she succumbed fatally, yielding first
of all to the purchases of a good housewife, then being
won over by attractive stylishness, and finally being
devoured"[22].

One may however note that this race, this struggle for
the consumer's money, has not been restricted to the
department stores, nor even to retail trade as a whole. It
extends today to all fields of human activity. Railway and
shipping companies, travel and tourist agencies, the electrical and automobile industries and many other branches of
economic life have entered the lists to ensure for themselves
as large a share as possible of the purchasing power of the
public.

More recently, an American sociologist, C. Wright Mills,
has commented as follows, on a higher plane, on the socio-

---

[21] F. Ambrière: "La vie secrète des grands magasins", Paris 1938,
p. 78.
[22] Emile Zola: "Notes de travail sur les grands magasins", Complete works, Volume 12, p. 467.

logical rôle of the department store: "In organizing the fetishism of commodities the Big Bazaar has made gods out of flux itself. Fashion used to be something for uptown aristocrats and had mainly to do with deities of dress. But the Big Bazaar has democratized the idea of fashion to all orders of commodities and for all classes of worshippers. Fashion means faster turnover, because if you worship the new, you will be ashamed of the old. In its benevolence, the Big Bazaar has built the rhythmic worship of fashion into the habits, and looks, and feelings of the urban mass: it has organized the imagination itself. In dressing people up and changing the scenery of their lives, on the street and in the bedroom, it has cultivated a great faith in the Religion of Appearance"[23].

The department store and real-estate values

If department stores have not always been in at the beginning of the creation of those districts which constitute the commercial centres of cities, they have, by their presence and development, assisted in raising the value of these centres and they have conferred upon them a much greater stability.

In the majority of cities, one finds in practice a main street or a group of main streets which represent the commercial heart of the community. There the majority of department stores and the best known specialty shops are grouped. There are, for example, Oxford Street in London, Fifth Avenue in New York, the Rue Neuve in Brussels, the Bahnhofstrasse in Zürich, Strøget in Copenhagen, the Kalverstraat in Amsterdam.

In Paris, one cannot properly speak of a single commercial centre, but rather of several commercial centres of which some are disposed round a department store.

There is no doubt that, by their presence and their development, the department stores have brought about a great increase in the value of the ground and the commercial sites, not only of the properties which they occupy, but also of the neighbouring properties, and even of the whole of

---

[23] C. Wright Mills: "White Collar—The American Middle Classes", New York 1951, pp. 168-169.

that part of the town in which they are situated. Their disappearance or even their decline would lead to a depreciation in real-estate values, which would amount to sums many times greater than the capital invested in the department stores themselves.

Furthermore, the department stores have not only contributed to set a value on real-estate: their existence has helped to give property values a greater degree of stability. These centres of commerce are not, of course, unalterable. In all the big cities it can be seen how the commercial centre tends to change its place. This migration is, for example, particularly striking in New York, where lower Fifth Avenue is losing its importance in favour of the upper end of the same thoroughfare. In Paris, the Louvre-Châtelet district lost its former importance in favour of the Opéra-St. Lazare district, and the latter in its turn lost part of its attraction to the Champs-Elysées quarter. But without the department stores, this migration of the commercial centres inside cities would be still more rapid and more marked than it is. The existence of the department stores assists in giving a greater stability to real-estate values and in preventing the migration of commercial centres, with the consequent depreciation in value, from being carried out at too rapid a pace.

The part played by the department stores in maintaining real-estate values, may be demonstrated by reference to any of the great cities. A typical example was pre-war Berlin. The extraordinary development of the west part of the town had affected the former commercial centre situated around the Leipziger and the Potsdamerstrasse. The experts of the Berlin property market asserted that only the existence in the old business quarter of the two department stores, Tietz and Wertheim, prevented a vertical fall in the value of the business established in this sector[24].

---

[24] M. Oxborn: "Stadt und Warenhaus, ein Beitrag zur boden- und baugeschichtlichen Entwicklung", Berlin 1928, p. 126.

VI

THE FUTURE OF THE DEPARTMENT STORE

IN this last chapter we intend to review the positive and negative aspects of the present-day department store and to consider in the broadest outline the nature of its problems and its capacity to meet the needs of the future.

The problems we have selected, each of which may well occupy a different place in the order of priorities and urgencies of the various stores, are, we believe, those which deserve particular attention.

As regards the measures proposed to overcome the corresponding difficulties, they consist, as will be seen, not in a servile imitation of the newer forms of distribution, but rather in efforts to grasp all the opportunities inherent in the make-up of the department store, so as to turn these natural assets to practical account.

Before proceeding, however, with this review we must try to outline the probable frame in which the department stores are going to operate and the new influences which are likely to be felt in the field of distribution. These underlying trends and these new forces coming to the surface are matters of profound significance, as we have reached a stage where, as noted by Hypps, more than 50 per cent. of the elements working for the success or failure of a business originate outside the enterprise.

Background

While it is not possible to determine with any accuracy the background against which the department store is going to operate in the coming decades, a few probable factors may nevertheless be singled out.

One may, for example, predict with certainty that motor car transportation will reach in Western Europe an even higher pitch of development than heretofore. The consequences of this trend will probably be similar to those noted in the United States during these last decades.

The greater mobility conferred by motor transportation will effect a redistribution of the population. This, coupled with the growing traffic congestion in the central areas of the largest cities, will give an added impetus to the development of auxiliary shopping centres in the suburbs and outskirts, and to automobile traffic along the periphery of the towns.

As regards the smaller cities, they will profit by the greater mobility of the country clientele. But in case the development of motor transportation by private cars is greatly expanded, one may experience the same phenomenon as in America, where the old established shopping districts in the centre of these towns are in some cases losing ground in favour of locations fringing the arterial roads towards the outskirts (like the sites of some of the Sears Roebuck and Montgomery Ward department stores). Another possible consequence of this increase in the general mobility of the public may be the revival on the outskirts of towns, of the market halls of former days, but under a new guise (such as that of the American supermarket).

The development of motor transportation is also likely to cause a growing substitution, in a number of great towns, of buses for tramcars (streetcars). Since bus-lines have a more flexible character than tramcars and as their routes are more easily and frequently changed, their development may help to give a less static character to the main shopping district and to the respective values of the different locations within this district.

It is also probable that a number of large towns will construct underground railways in order to relieve the traffic congestion above the surface. The location of these underground lines, and especially of their stations, may considerably affect the respective value of the locations of the existing department stores.

The same may be said of the new traffic lanes which may be opened or enlarged in conjunction with town replanning schemes, or of the possible change in the location of those railway stations which handle the suburban traffic.

The probable great expansion of aviation in the decades to come is also likely to influence department stores, specially if the development of the helicopter can bring people directly to the business centres.

In that case, as prophesied by Sir Woodman Burbidge, important provincial towns may become suburbs of the capital of the country; a number of people living in the great provincial towns may get the habit of coming by air for shopping in the capital, returning home on the same day.

It may be noted that the development of the telephone technique for trunk or long distance calls may work in the same direction. The fact that a long distance call will be obtained directly, i.e., without the subscriber having to be recalled, as well as the probable extension of the direct dial call system to the whole country, may sponsor telephone shopping at department stores from the whole country, especially at those which have the greatest prestige, the metropolitan stores.

In fact, the two developments which we have just considered (aviation and telephone) may help to give to department stores, or to some department stores, a market which will extend to the whole country rather than to a city area.

Such an extension of the market of the metropolitan department stores would, of course, require an adaptation of their sales promotion and even merchandising methods. It is probable that the extension of the market of metropolitan department stores to the whole country as a result of the development of aviation will refer mainly to department stores catering for a high income level clientele. On the other hand, the extension of the market to the whole country by means of the telephone might be perfectly conceivable for department stores catering for a middle class clientele.

Another technical development which may, on the whole favourably affect the prospects of department stores, is represented by the development of television. It may be that in the use of television for publicity purposes department stores will be at an advantage over many other forms of retailing, on account of their resources, volume of sales, variety of lines carried, and their rôle of greatest fashion distributors.

Another and more general aspect of technical progress, the growing development, thanks to industrial research, of new materials, has to be mentioned here, as it may bring a greater degree of transference and mutation in assortment and resources. It may, however, be noted that department stores, thanks to their elaborate merchandising organization, are in a better position than many other forms of retailing to watch closely the results of such research, and rapidly to take profit from it.

As the department store has always reflected the social changes of the time we find it not out of place to consider also the future from this angle. As a matter of fact, no discussion of economic forces can be altogether isolated from the social question.

The reduction in number of the members of the highest income group and the decrease of their resources under the conjugated action of increasing taxation, governmental controls and development of the public sector of the national economy, is an already acknowledged fact; and this trend is likely to continue in the future, thus obliging those stores which have catered until now for a high income clientele to extend their trade to the middle class.

Another, one may say opposite, movement also deserves to be considered. It is the trend towards a relative reduction of the numerical force of the working class (in the sense of an industrial proletariat) and a reinforcement of the lower middle class. This evolution is the result of the simultaneous force of several factors, such as new social conceptions, growing state ownership, the power of organized labour, the diffusion of education, growing mechanization, etc. One can see the result of this development in America, where, in spite of the high degree of industrialization, the middle class is as numerous as the working class, because an appreciable part of the working class has reached a standard of life which brings it into the middle class. It is not unlikely that a similar movement will take place in the most advanced European countries. If this is the case, the implications of such a transformation on the orientation of department store trade may be considerable. This would mean that, as is already the case in

America and to a certain extent in Scandinavia, the department stores which represent the greatest sales volumes will not be those which cover the popular class, but those which cater for the middle class.

It is, on the other hand, certain that we shall experience a continuation and a precipitation of the process which changes the status of an article from a luxury to a necessity. We have, for example, witnessed the development of the production of furniture, well within the reach of everybody, and we believe that such production will continue and even expand. The previous situation, where the majority of the furniture manufacturers made expensive suites while the market for cheap furniture was badly covered, was irrational and against the spirit of the time.

Another trend which has to be recorded is the growing expenditure of the state and of public bodies. In a great number of fields the state has a tendency to take over functions which were previously performed by the individual consumer, with a corresponding displacement of the place and methods of buying. We do not think that this displacement is as unfavourable to department stores as to the small retailer, since public bodies are more inclined to do business with big organizations. But one must also consider the inclination of these large-scale purchasers to short-circuit completely the retail trade and to buy directly from the wholesaler or the manufacturer. Department stores may possess the advantage of meeting this growing demand by providing suitable discounts and an adequate organization to cope with their sales to institutions, as distinct from their ordinary sales to individual customers.

Competition

It is advisable to review here the competitive channels of distribution which the department stores will have to consider during the coming years, in order to see in their true light and proportion the real forces they will have to face.

Beginning with the small independent retailer, it is probable that the creation of voluntary chains and the general popularization of rationalization will bring an improvement in operating methods in this field. The con-

tinuous development of national brands and of the practice
of fixed resale prices will also be of benefit to this form of
distribution. But we do not believe that this reinforcement
of the small shopkeeper will be detrimental to department
stores: rather the contrary. Furthermore, the majority
of these small independent retailers represent neighbourhood stores located in the various sections of the town
and drawing their trade from people living close at hand;
they sell mainly convenience goods, i.e., goods bought
without comparison between several stores, whilst the bulk
of the trade of department stores is made up of shopping
goods, i.e., articles which are bought only after a comparison
of price, style and quality.

From this point of view the specialty stores located, as
are the department stores, in the central shopping district
of the town, represent a more dangerous antagonist. Their
advantages are well-known. The most valuable is probably
the higher quality of their sales force. The direct contact
between the owner or manager and the staff and the public,
is also one of their superiorities. Furthermore, as already
stated, these specialty stores seem to have taken more than
one leaf from the book of large-scale retailing, especially
in the field of modern methods of merchandising, display
and promotion. On the other hand, their disadvantages are:
relatively much higher rentals than department stores;
their reduced size which does not allow them to use modern
sales promotion methods effectively, to grant services to
the customers economically, to profit by the savings of
large-scale operation (this refers especially to the operation
of the non-selling departments) or to hire highly qualified
and relatively expensive specialized executives.

The specialty chains may be deemed a more dangerous
opponent to the department store. Their advantages and
superiorities have already been listed in the corresponding
paragraph of a preceding chapter. Their great development
during the last decades is the best proof of their strength,
mainly based on the mass buying of standardized merchandise. From a number of standpoints one may consider them
as better adapted than department stores to the economic
distribution of merchandise on a large scale. There have

always been stores underselling department stores. But these were shabby establishments offering merchandise of very inferior quality. With the specialty chain has appeared, on the contrary, a new form of competition often selling merchandise of comparable quality at a lower price than department stores, and this in up-to-date premises. It has already demonstrated in a number of countries the measure of its striking power.

But the dark side of the picture should not be over-stressed. It is thus only fair to list some of the disadvantages of the specialty chain as compared with the department store. Its rentals are usually markedly higher than those of the department store (often 10 per cent. or more, as against an average rental—or rather real-estate cost—of about four per cent. in department stores). The level of their selling staff is also generally distinctly inferior to that of the specialty store and, on the whole, lower than that of department store personnel. This lower level in staff is a general characteristic of the chain stores. For the majority of chain stores which sell convenience goods it is not a great inconvenience. But for the specialty chains which are primarily selling shopping goods it is a great handicap.

One must also consider that it is mainly in the field of mass buying, standardized assortment, etc., that the specialty chain is able to ensure the advantages of large-scale operation. On the other hand, in numerous other directions, as for example the various forms of services to customers, the education of the personnel, a number of non-selling activities, and even in the field of sales promotion, it is at a disadvantage, as compared with the department store, on account of the relatively limited size of each selling unit. In fact, the chain store can neither have the unity nor the personality of the department store. To most customers the unit in the chain is just a small shop, even if they do know that it is the unit of a huge chain. The emotional impression they get cannot be the same as the one they feel when they enter the large building of a department store[1].

[1] E. Filene: "Next Steps Forward in Retailing", New York 1937, p. 60.

One must also note that the branch of the specialty chain has usually less local 'anchorage' in the community than the individual department store. It purchases less locally, contributes less to local charities, does not live to the same degree the life of the community, and has in general a smaller hold on the imagination of the public than the department store.

The specialty chain is finally not in as favourable a position as the department store to exploit the fashion factor, and this on two counts. First because the existence of related groups of merchandise in department stores is a great advantage in ascertaining and promoting fashions. Secondly because for merchandise where style and fashion play a great rôle, the consumer demand must be first ascertained by trials before making great commitments. It must, however, be admitted, as regards this last point, that the methods developed by some specialty chains, with a stringent application of statistical merchandise control to determine customer preferences may, as already stated, help to bring fashion articles within the reach of central buying and central merchandising. Such a development would also be of a great advantage to the chain of department stores, but it would mainly reinforce the possibilities of the specialty chain against the individually operated department store.

From the unit price stores, with their tremendous buying power for standardized merchandise, the danger lies, as already seen, not so much in their hold on the articles of lowest unit price (the former threepenny and sixpenny lines), but their expansion to higher price lines. There is no doubt that the creation of a chain of the type of Marks and Spencer Limited has represented most serious competition for department stores, especially those catering for the low income class clientele.

Even when extending their assortment to articles of a higher unit value, the unit price stores, or rather the variety chains as they are now called, have continued to play the economic and social rôle which was theirs since their creation and which we have already described as bringing "shopping" within the reach of every pocket.

In fact, the modern variety chain may be considered as the very embodiment in the field of distribution of the main tendencies of our time, i.e., the stress on planning, organization, standardization, centralized control, and the reduction of the scope of the work of the operative (in this case the sales assistant) by a transfer of skill to special centralized agencies. What have hitherto been considered the very foundations of commerce, namely salesmanship and advertising, are fading out in the variety chain, because the commercial factor is, so to speak, built-in in the merchandise (creative and sometimes high pressure merchandising), in the fixtures (the system of display), and in the lighting (which in its modern form of fluorescent lighting of high intensity replaces, within certain limits, and under a new form, high pressure salesmanship).

We have already pointed out how the department store had been operated, since its very creation, on the strength of a new principle, the principle of fixed and marked prices, and how this principle was in reality the consequence of the assumption that in such large enterprises bargaining could not be left in the hands of the sales assistant. The unit price store has represented one step further in this evolution, with salesmanship itself being to a considerable degree taken out of the hands of the salesman.

Continuing our review of the probable competitive position of department stores, we must note that the co-operative societies, which are very developed in Great Britain, the Low Countries, the Scandinavian countries and Switzerland, and which will probably re-appear in Germany and Italy, have had during the last decades a tendency to penetrate into lines of merchandise other than the food trade on which they previously concentrated. The expansion of the co-operatives in the field of clothing and home furnishings may provide additional competition for department stores, especially for those catering for a popular clientele. This movement has already resulted in the operation, by the co-operatives, of a few full-size department stores.

One may say in general that in the years to come the department store will come into conflict with a number of elements, among which the specialty chains and the unit price stores, provided they are allowed to develop freely, are probably the most potent.

The old array of forces has been scattered, and a new range appears. What was previously a duel between small independent retailers and department stores has become a triangular contest between the new forms of retailing, the department stores and the remainder of the trade.

And, superimposed on this struggle between the different forms of retailing, we must expect the continuation and aggravation of another fight, the fight for the consumers' money between different lines of human activity. This has already been felt during the last decades, for example by the popularization of the automobile, the growing expenditure on sports, travel, education, recreation, etc. This fight has assumed the aspect of a contest of great magnitude and portent. One may assume that it will upset many preconceived ideas and raise new issues which might well alter the very essence of the problem of competition. It is at any rate certain that the shift of emphasis from merchandise to services will be even greater during the decades to come. As a matter of fact, the shortening of the working day will favour the spending of the income in these directions. This will result in a situation where the total retail sales will show appreciably smaller yearly increases than the national income or the total of consumers' expenditure.

Regulation

It is difficult to predict to what extent, under the effect of political pressure, legislative regulations are going to interfere with the free play of natural economic forces, in the field of business, and especially distribution.

It is possible that the same trend which we have noticed during the thirties will continue in America and in the countries of Western and Northern Europe. This means that we will move in retailing, as in other aspects of business, towards something resembling the medieval organization of trade, with an emphasis upon security and stability rather than upon freedom and progress[2].

---

[2] Report of a lecture by Ralph M. Hower: "Retailing", New York, April 3, 1939, p. 16.

If this is the case the natural development of the newer forms of retailing represented by the unit price stores and the chain stores is going to be artificially prevented. As regards the department stores this would probably mean a continuation and extension of the regulation introduced in several European countries prohibiting the opening of new department stores and the enlargement of existing ones, as well as the existence of a special taxation.

In fact, when one considers the great potentialities of the specialty chains and of the unit price stores, one may come to the conclusion that such a movement for the regulation of trade will in a way be favourable for the department store, unless it takes the form of excessive discriminatory taxation, as its main effect will be to prevent these new forms of distribution from reaching, at the expense of department stores, the great expansion which would be theirs in a regime of full liberty.

But it is evident that this is a negative approach to our problem. A constructive form of business such as the department store owes it to its past to rely for its future not on artificial protection but on its own forces. The argument offered in this chapter will thus mainly centre on the means which are likely to allow a profitable operation of department stores, vis-à-vis all the other forms of distribution, including the specialty chain and the unit price store.

We must, however, also take into consideration the extreme and unlikely case where, as a result of political pressure and demagogic agitation, a prohibitive taxation might be imposed on department stores in some countries. Should this occur, the only way to make possible a continuation of the activity of the firms and a preservation of the experience embodied in that form of business, would consist in the transformation of former department stores into wholesale organizations of a new type, which would not only perform a job of central buying for smaller retailers, but would also develop an extended activity of consulting work in matters of merchandising, sales promotion, advertising, display and store management.

This would be an evolution offering some similarity to that noted in America, where, as a result of increasing taxation, a number of chain stores have transformed themselves into voluntary chains, their former central organs playing the rôle of the wholesaler and consultant for the branches, these having become independent stores. A similar transformation might be conceivable for department stores in some circumstances. It would be warranted by the great amount of expert knowledge embodied in these institutions, and would certainly be to the benefit of those retail shops which would be supplied and serviced by these former department stores.

In the case of the great chains of department stores with powerful central buying organizations already supplying many affiliated stores, this evolution would not be difficult to achieve. In other cases, it would require an entirely new set-up.

Class of trade

In discussing the future of the department store the question of the class of trade is the logical starting point, as we find this problem interlocked with every other issue. It is a fundamental question in the sense that if we go wrong in it everything else will automatically go wrong. This question, which must thus have the first call on our attention, may be put as follows: Assuming that the new forms of large-scale retailing, represented by the unit price stores and the specialty chains will be allowed to develop freely, must those department stores which at present cater for a popular or popular-to-middle class clientele stay in their present class of trade, or must they, on the contrary, try to trade up and to abandon the bulk of the popular trade to these new forms of large-scale retailing?

It must first be noted that the only way department stores could compete with these new forms of retailing in the lower end of the trade would consist in taking over most of the latter's characteristics—mass purchasing, a great measure of standardization of the assortment, a greater standardization in the selling operations and a smaller amount of service granted to the customer.

There is certainly a place for the department store in this field, but as the major condition for the successful operation in such a line is large-scale purchasing, we believe that only the great chains of department stores will, in the long run, be able to cover successfully that part of the trade.

With the other department stores (the individually operated department stores and even the chains with only a few units) it is probable that those who cater for the popular clientele and are operated in countries where the new forms of distribution are allowed to expand, are going to trade up.

There is no doubt that at first sight this evolution seems to be illogical if one considers that trading up brings an increase of the expense percentage of a store; for stores catering for a higher income level clientele have greater expenses than those catering for a clientele of a lower income class. One could thus criticize this evolution from the following point of view: the department stores finding that their cost of distribution is too high to compete with the new forms of distribution, answer by taking a measure which inevitably causes a further increase in their cost of distribution.

If, in spite of this apparent inconsistency, department stores have in several countries followed such a trend, it is because they have felt that it was very difficult for them to compete on price appeal with the new forms of distribution, and that it was preferable to penetrate into income levels where the fashion or service appeal plays a greater rôle.

It seems clear that this trend is going to continue and that a certain degree of division of labour will take place in large-scale retailing (always provided that a régime of liberty of commerce allows the new forms of retailing to take their full development).

The need for economy and low cost distribution will be covered by the chain stores, the unit price stores, as well as by the great department store chains, rather than (as was the case in former days) by the department stores.

On the other hand, the typical department store—the individually operated department store or the chain of department stores of a few units—will rather meet the need for customer convenience, variety of choice, fashion and services, which correspond to the desires and means of the middle class[3].

To foresee such an evolution, such a difference in motive and design, consists simply in recognizing the fact that the typical department store has lost its former advantage of being the most economic form of distribution: the advantages of mass buying and more economic operation are now in the hands of newer forms of distribution, which include the large chains of department stores.

Yet the typical department store has still its advantages, as, for example, its greater unit size, its greater convenience for customers, its reputation for fashion, its ability to offer wider service. All these factors represent powerful elements of customer attraction; but they involve higher expenses and can probably be maintained only by abandoning the lower end of the trade.

At first sight such a course indicates that most department stores will forego what will probably be the great opportunity of the future, the raising of the standard of life of the masses. But there are other trends which will be not unfavourable to stores catering for the middle class clientele.

We have already pointed out that, in our opinion, future social evolution will, in a number of European countries, tend towards a situation similar to that existing already in the United States, where, in spite of the high degree of industrialization, the middle class is gaining ground at the expense of the working class (in the sense of the industrial proletariat), because a growing number of workers are attaining the standard of life of the middle class.

It may be noted that for such people, who climb a few rungs up the social ladder and who leave the working class proper to penetrate into the middle class at its lower end, the department store has often represented the most convenient and effective means of introduction to a new way of life. The members of such families, or their offspring, abandon some of the stores which they formerly patronized,

---

[3] See Report on a lecture by Ralph M. Hower, "Retailing", April 3, 1939, p. 16.

not for the specialty stores of the central shopping district of the town (the jump would be too great and the atmosphere of such stores is often uncongenial or embarrassing for them) but for the department stores located in the same central shopping district. And even when they are contented customers of the variety chains they are likely to transfer part of their purchases to department stores. For a number of articles they are prepared to pay a price merely in order to buy the same or a comparable article in the more dignified atmosphere of the department store, provided this extra charge is not unreasonable.

In catering for the middle class the department store will find still other opportunities. Everybody knows that process which the unit price stores have so successfully developed, whereby an article hitherto belonging to the assortment supplied to the middle class is made available to the great mass of the public.

A similar field is open, on the next level, to the department store. One of its activities must consist in changing the status of certain articles which have been considered as luxuries in the sense that they have belonged to the highest income class, so as to make them available to the middle class, perhaps in some cases by means of co-operative purchases by a group of department stores.

The department store chains

In foreseeing for the department store a tendency to trade up and thus to abandon, in face of the competition of the new forms of distribution, the market of the most popular class, we were considering only the singly operated department store and the department store chain of a few units.

The large chains of department stores (and as already recorded there has been during recent decades a tendency toward the formation and expansion of these large groups of stores) are on the contrary well suited to cover the popular clientele, and are equipped with the weapon, large-scale purchasing, which makes it possible to fight the new forms of distribution on their own ground.

Past experience has moreover shown that the operation of a chain of department stores effectively practising central buying and central merchandising, is most profitable in enterprises catering for a popular clientele, since the corresponding assortment is better adapted to that standardization which makes it possible for central buying and central merchandising to achieve its full effect. As a matter of fact, the chains of department stores which have brought the practice of central buying and central merchandising to its highest pitch of efficiency are enterprises like Sears Roebuck, Montgomery Ward and Penney in America, Lewis's Ltd. in Great Britain, the Printemps in France, the Westdeutsche Kaufhof in Germany and the Innovation in Belgium, all of which cater for a popular clientele.

One has thus every reason to believe that the large chains of department stores will be able to hold their own in face of the competition presented by the new forms of retailing. It is possible that they may have to yield some ground in the sales of smallwares, but great opportunities lie open for them in other sections of the assortment, mainly perhaps in the home furnishing division. One of the missions of the large department store chains will consist in doing for these articles what the unit price store has done for small articles, viz., to realize by mass purchasing, creative merchandising and simplification that price decrease which will bring new articles within the reach of the popular classes.

All these considerations refer to the chains of department stores catering for the popular class. For those catering for a clientele of a level above the lowest class, the possibilities of central buying and central merchandising have been until now more limited and have mainly centred on staple and semi-staple merchandise such as ladies' and girls' underlinen, sheetings, blankets, bedding, curtains, hosiery, hardware, chinaware, men's clothing, inexpensive dresses, certain kinds of piece goods, etc., and not on fashion goods[4]. As a matter of fact, the chains of department stores catering for a middle or high income class clientele

---

[4] See W. Gabler: "Probleme der amerikanischen Warenhäuser", Zürich 1934, p. 178.

do not usually fully utilize the principle of central buying and central merchandising. There are, however, even in this category of stores, some remarkable advances in the direction of central buying and central merchandising.

One must also take into consideration the fact that some American specialty chains have developed, on the basis of the use of statistical merchandise control, new methods of operation which seem to bring fashion articles within the reach of central buying and central merchandising.

One knows at any rate that Filene has predicted a great future for the chain of department stores which, in his opinion, will represent one day the most perfect form of distribution, combining the economy of the chain store and its mass purchasing with the advantages of the department store, its greater personality, its shopping convenience and its large-scale organization of services.

He has also expressed the opinion that the chain of department stores will not, in the future, be confined to the popular class clientele, but will also take a dominant position in the trade catering for the middle class.

Trends in the evolution of the location and structure of retail units

When observing the evolution of the location and structure of retail units, one may assert that the most striking and original development in recent years has been the emergence and expansion of the so-called supermarkets in the United States. In spite of the fact that they increasingly develop their non-food lines of merchandise, they belong basically to the food trade, that is to say, a line in which the department store has only a secondary interest.

But this development of the supermarket nevertheless deserves to be considered, because it outlines directions along which the distribution structures of the future may tend to move.

It reveals first of all, by the location of these supermarkets in the different sections of the towns, and especially the suburbs, a tendency towards decentralization.

But from the point of view of the department store the most interesting feature of this new development lies in another characteristic of the supermarkets, namely the relative large unit size of these stores, and, especially, the fact that they include a variety of lines of merchandise, a variety which tends still to grow. This development, which is actually one of the most significant of recent years, tends to show that the movement of decentralization of retail centres takes the form of relatively large units where various lines of merchandise are gathered under one roof.

Thus while this trend may appear contrary to the immediate interests of department stores, in that these are mostly concentrated in the central shopping districts, it also takes a form, the gathering of different lines of trade under one roof, which is the very essence of the form of distribution represented by the department store itself.

Suburban branches

The continuous development of the outskirts of the largest towns, due to the expansion and overcrowding of cities and to the desire for cheaper and more healthy living conditions, has resulted in the creation of important residential suburbs or satellite agglomerations. This trend is likely to continue and even to become more marked during the coming decades.

This tendency, coupled with the growing traffic difficulties in the central shopping districts, will not only set limits to the possibilities of enlargement of the metropolitan department stores, but will also actively favour the growth of secondary shopping centres in the suburbs. This shifting of the population to the suburban areas has already resulted in the formation of outlying retail centres, with consequences dangerous to the department stores.

The location of department stores in the central shopping district has often precluded the possibility of securing a large amount of the convenience goods business. The development of these suburban shopping districts has now begun to affect the part of the trade where department stores hitherto have had a firm hold, namely the sale of shopping goods.

It might be a sound move for the department stores located in the largest metropolitan areas to open suburban branches in these outlying retail districts. This policy has been followed during the last decades by a number of American department stores and has given rise to a new type of department store, the suburban branch.

These small department stores are now well-known, for example, in the regions of New York, Boston, Cleveland, Chicago, Los Angeles. They are remarkable for their pleasant appearance, well-arranged layout, modern fixtures, convenient interior display.

This establishment of suburban branches has, of course, the disadvantage of strengthening the power of attraction of the suburban shopping districts. By establishing a branch in such a suburban shopping district a metropolitan department store lends to it its prestige and contributes thus to the building up of a competitive centre of retailing. It has been said that department stores cut their own throats by the establishment of suburban branches which strengthen these outlying shopping sections.

But the problem may be viewed from a wider angle. If the development of these suburban shopping districts is inevitable, it is preferable for the department store to participate in and profit by their development. It is, in fact, the policy which has been followed by a number of Continental department stores in relation to the unit price stores, and one may say that such a policy represents the most constructive approach to the problem. It recognizes facts and tries to adapt the operation of the firm to these facts, even at the cost of a possible future transformation of the character of the business, a transformation which may be made inevitable by the evolution of the forms of re-tailing.

One must, however, keep in mind the fact that this American development is based primarily upon an expansion of the motoring habit on a scale still unknown in Europe where motoring, while making continuous progress, has not yet become, as it has in the United States, an essential feature of everyday life. Thus these American suburban branches are for the most part placed not in the outskirts proper of a large city, but rather in satellite small towns located 10 or more miles away from the central shopping district of the main town. There is already here a structure of town planning and development strongly influenced by motoring, and hardly to be found in Europe. Furthermore, these small satellite centres where the suburban branches of the department stores are located are usually too small to warrant by themselves the operation of a department store, even of reduced size. These suburban branches, and the corresponding shopping centres, obtain in reality a sufficient volume of sales only because they can attract, thanks again to the general habit of going everywhere by car, the patronage of inhabitants of other satellite towns placed in the same area but in a relatively wide circle; for these people the alternative is often a 10-minute drive to the suburban branch with plenty of parking facilities or a 40-minute drive to the congested central shopping centre with no parking space available. Such developments are hardly conceivable in Europe, where most customers have to rely on public transport facilities, these being nearly always laid out with the central shopping district of the main town as the hub of the system, and with the lateral or peripherical communications very poorly developed.

In the large European towns the location of such suburban branches would have to be different: they would have to be placed not in distant satellite cities, but rather at focal points situated at the limit where the city proper ends and the suburbs start.

Departmentalization for the customer

As is known, the department store is the most concentrated type of retail enterprise. The grouping of several merchandise lines under the same roof has been for the department store, since its inception, the primary instrument of its growth. And this phenomenon of mutual support of different merchandise lines, as a consequence of the gathering together in the same store of various categories of articles, is as strong as ever. Indeed, new factors such as the growing traffic congestion in the central shopping districts, the adoption of escalators, the increased importance of the factor fashion, contribute to make this characteristic of department stores even more valuable than in former days. It is to be noted, moreover, that (with the possible exception of the unit price store) the department store is the only form of distribution which has this advantage at its disposal.

In accordance with that major principle of business strategy which consists in playing on its own strong points, the department store must concentrate part of its efforts on this characteristic and try to exploit fully all its implications.

From this point of view, the studies of Dr. Charles H. Wahl in which he suggested a new composition of the selling departments, with the merchandise mainly grouped according to the use made of the articles by the customer, and not according to the traditional principles found in retail trade, deserve to be seriously reconsidered. The grouping of the men's departments and of the children's departments has already been carried out in a number of department stores with complete success. There are, besides these, a great number of other possibilities, as for example the grouping of the accessories with the corresponding outer garments, the reclassification of the piece goods and regrouping of related goods within the home furnishing group according to actual domestic usage.

In spite of the difficulties and transformations such a step would entail, one must keep in mind that this approach is basically sound, as it achieves a double purpose: it increases customer convenience (perhaps not immediately but in the long run) and while doing this it leads the department store in a direction where the competition from the remainder of the retail trade cannot follow it.

Such an action follows the path which department stores must take in the present circumstances where, in face of newer and, on the whole, more economic forms of distribution, they can hope to hold their own, not by a servile imitation, but on the contrary by developing all the potentialities of their own form of distribution.

We are inclined to consider this approach as an outstanding factor in the possible reinforcement of the position of department stores. By means of this departmentalization based on related needs, a new and great force of customer attraction can be brought into play.

Relative development of merchandise lines

Considering this problem from a long-term point of view, one may predict that the shifts in customer demand which characterized the period 1920-1940 are going to continue, and perhaps to be amplified, during the coming decades.

These trends are mainly characterized by a decline in the department store's relative share of the sales in the clothing, piece goods and soft furnishings lines, and an increase in the relative share of lines like toilet requisites, household and medical supplies, medical apparatus, electrical and other household appliances, including radio and television sets, toys, sporting equipment, travelling requisites and hardware articles.

The evolution of total retail sales in general has been in the preceding decades (and is likely to continue to be) from the so-called 'soft' goods to the so-called 'hard' lines. Within the 'soft' goods group itself one may note the progress of informal clothing. It would be wise for department stores to take this evolution into consideration by expanding or creating the corresponding departments.

It is especially important to note that electrical household appliances are passing the stage where door-to-door personal selling represented the major share of the trade: they have reached the so-called acceptance stage where a real demand, finding its way to the stores, has been created.

Purchase terms and quantity discounts

The securing of lower purchase prices than the majority of other retailers has been, and remains, one of the assets of department stores.

These lower purchase terms are granted by manufacturers or wholesalers to department stores, either on account of their larger purchases or by reason of that standing and reputation which makes department stores desirable distributors, conferring on the products they launch or carry a certain element of prestige.

When considering objectively the position of the department store in relation to this important factor, one cannot but come to the conclusion that the situation is not without dangers.

First one may note that the actual justification of these lower purchase prices on account of the volume of the merchandise bought is really present only for a minority of stores, namely the chains of department stores which practise central buying, or some very large individually operated department stores which reach in several of their merchandise categories volumes of sales many times superior to those of the typical store in this field.

But the future development of specialty chains, unit price stores and of voluntary chains may produce concentrations of buying power in definite lines of merchandise equal to those of the greatest department store chains and vastly superior to those of the majority of individually operated department stores. In fact, the average department store is, as regards buying, not a large-scale establishment, but a collection of selling departments in each of which retailing is carried out on a relatively small scale.

It may be remarked that Filene has gone so far as to explain the great attention usually attached in department stores to merchandising and buying, with the relative neglect of other functions, precisely by the fact that, as the department stores are small-scale establishments from the point of view of the quantity of merchandise purchased, they are obliged to compensate for that inherent weakness by giving much attention and by devoting much time to the work of merchandising and buying; firstly because they have to buy thousands of different articles, and this always in relatively small quantities; and secondly because they have to use all kinds of painstaking merchandising and buying devices—and sometimes even tricks—to secure those price advantages that the newer forms of distribution secure naturally by their mass purchases.

In fact, when department stores do receive price concessions from the supplier, these derive in several cases from a cause not connected with the volume of their purchases but with another factor: the standing and reputation of the department store, its publicity value for the manufacturer.

But this is a somewhat dangerous element, since it is based less on economic factors than on intangible values. It will maintain itself as long as the department stores retain much of their prestige, but it may disappear one day. Moreover, in at least one country, namely the United States, legislative stipulations have been put into force (directed, it is true, mainly against chain stores, but which may also one day be turned against department stores), prohibiting manufacturers and wholesalers from giving to their customers price discounts which are not strictly based on the savings of large orders demonstrable by cost accounting calculation.

While the chains of department stores will probably, from this point of view, keep their ground whatever the future evolution, it is possible that the individually operated department stores will be increasingly obliged to create co-operative joint buying organizations composed of non-competing stores located in different cities in order to obtain favourable purchase terms, not necessarily for the majority of the items of their assortment but for some key items.

Mark-up and pricing

As the retailer is a merchant not only of goods but also of prices, the question of mark-up and pricing deserves careful attention. Two well-known experts on retailing, McNair and Törnqvist, have attached the greatest import-ance to this problem, and are inclined to explain the present relative weakness of the department stores by their too primitive or faulty practices as regards mark-up determina-tion and pricing.

McNair has noted the advantages of modern methods of merchandising control whereby, for example, the mark-up of each selling department (and even each sub-division) is planned in advance, and maximum and minimum rates of initial mark-up, within which the buyer has to set the price of the merchandise, are imposed. But he has pointed out a weakness which has resulted from this practice or from its exaggeration, namely too great a uniformity in mark-up: "Control mechanisms clearly have their place in department stores, but they must be subordinated to sound merchandise skill and imagination. One of their bad results has been for example the effort to achieve too great a uniformity in mark-up with a corresponding over-rigid thinking"[5].

Törnqvist has approached the question from another and wider angle, and the conclusions of his outstanding investigation deserve, on account of their consequences, to be reproduced here.

Considering the success of the unit price stores, and the progress of this important commercial experiment, perhaps the most logical and complete yet tried in the field of distribution, he has stated that the great development of unit price stores is due to certain features which are well-known, but the origin and implications of which are usually not fully grasped by department store people.

One of the characteristics of unit price stores lies, of course, in the fact that they select their assortment so as to carry only articles which have a high rate of stockturn and which necessitate a minimum of sales talk and of selling service. Another of their main features is to present all the merchandise in the form of open, classified, displays.

The combination of these two factors has allowed a great simplification, to the point of a revolution, in the selling work. Part of the work of the sales assistant is suppressed or transferred to the customer.

The unit price stores have thus concentrated their assortment exclusively on those articles which have the cheapest selling expenses (i.e., articles which require a minimum of selling work and which have the highest rate of stockturn) and have obtained a correspondingly low gross margin.

But their success would not have been as great if they had not profited from a weakness common to the whole retail trade, including the department stores, namely the total neglect of the fact that the various articles of the assortment have very different selling expenses. Department stores, following the example of the retail trade at large, determine the mark-up of the articles they sell on the basis of the purchase cost, the average gross margin of

---

[5] M. P. McNair: "Trends in large-scale retailing". Harvard Business Review, October 1931.

the department, competitors' prices and sometimes also the rate of mark-downs in that category of articles; but they do not take into consideration the selling expenses of the article. These selling expenses depend mainly upon the rate of stockturn of the article; the average duration of the transaction for selling that article; and, also, the average portion of the selling time spent on 'not concluded' sales for that category of articles. These three main factors[6] which may vary quite widely for the different articles composing the assortment of the same merchandise group, are hardly ever taken into consideration in pricing the merchandise.

Törnqvist says it is this irrational character of the mark-up rates of retail trade, including department stores, which has contributed towards the great development of the unit price store[7]. It is on account of their crude mark-up methods that department stores have presented an easy target to the attacks of the unit price stores, and have been ill-prepared to resist their onslaught. In their ignorance of the real cost of selling the various categories of articles of their assortment department stores use a rate of mark-up which is too uniform, often charging a mark-up relatively too inflated on those articles which have the highest rate of stockturn and the shortest average duration of transaction, and a relatively too low mark-up on those articles which have the lowest rate of stockturn and the longest average duration of transaction.

This situation has existed for years without producing too great drawbacks, as a compensation has usually occurred between the part of the assortment marked at a mark-up relatively too low (i.e., relative to the actual selling expenses of these articles) and the part marked at a relatively too high mark-up. But one day a new form of distribution appeared—the unit price store—whose whole success was based precisely on this weakness. It built its assortment by selecting only those articles with the smallest

---

[6] To which one might perhaps add two others, namely the proportion of 'send' transactions and the average delivery expenses for that category of articles.

[7] G. Törnqvist: "Detaljhandelns Stordriftsformer", Stockholm 1936, pp. 23-24.

selling expenses (the highest rate of stockturn and the shortest average duration of the transaction), and presented those articles at their true mark-up. It is this development which has brought this fundamental weakness of the department store sharply into focus.

The conclusion to be drawn from these considerations is that the development of more rational methods of mark-up determination and of pricing, based on the difference in actual selling expense existing between the different categories of articles which constitute the assortment of a department, is one of the important problems department stores have to tackle if they wish to be favourably situated in a trial of strength with the new forms of retailing.

Thanks to their research departments and to the expert knowledge they have accumulated in these questions of cost allocation and determination, department stores are in a better position than any other form of retailing to handle this problem. Any advances made in this direction will reinforce their ability to compete with the new forms of distribution represented by the unit price stores and the chain stores. It is true that such a move would result in decreases in mark-up for some articles; but it would result also in increases of mark-up for others. Moreover, the increases of mark-up would refer mainly to merchandise in which the department stores set the tone for the whole retail trade, whilst the decreases in mark-up would mostly affect merchandise lines where the department stores are obliged to fight against the newer forms of retailing.

Further, the possession of the basic information represented by the difference in selling expenses existing between different articles would, for the first time, place at the disposal of department stores the evidence enabling them to perform on the basis of facts and not, as until now, in the dark, that capital function of merchandising which consists in suggesting additions to or deductions from the assortment in order to realize greater profits.

In fact, the whole future of the department store may be conditioned by the fundamental re-alignment brought about by the determination of the different selling cost of various items of the assortment. The task is unexampled of its kind. But it is a problem which may one day dominate all others. It may well be that if department stores can settle this problem they can settle everything else; if they cannot settle it they can settle nothing.

Creative merchandising

The development of the practice of creative merchandising and the substitution of creative merchandising for mere high pressure merchandising is one of the great questions department stores have to face.

We have already defined 'high pressure merchandising', a companion to high pressure sales promotion, as the tendency to decrease the price of articles just by lessening their quality, while maintaining, as far as possible, their former appearance.

Creative merchandising represents a more positive approach to that new mission of distribution where the retailer does not confine himself to the rôle of a mere distributor of goods, but contributes to the creation, development and design of the merchandise to be sold.

Creative merchandising may take a great number of different forms, among which are these: inspiration of the manufacturer by influencing him in the design of the articles as regards size, shape, colour, material, price, etc.; original creation and design of articles by the store; co-operation with the manufacturer in new developments and experiments; alteration of the design of articles to make them exclusive to the store; study of novelties, especially those of foreign origin, with the purpose of suggesting them to national manufacturers; a study of possible modifications and simplifications in order to make the product available at lower prices; designing, redesigning, changing or improving the packing of the articles; development of store brands[8].

It must be admitted that some aspects of creative merchandising, as for example the study of possible modifications

---

[8] Examples of various forms of creative merchandising were given by E. J. B. Lloyd in an address presented at a meeting of the Royal Society of Arts, London on April 30th, 1947, and by R. Kalderén in an address at the Design Congress, London in September 1951.

and simplifications, in order to make it possible to offer an article at a lower price, may come pretty near to that practice of high pressure merchandising which we have criticized. But there is in reality, even in this borderline case, a difference between creative and high pressure merchandising which derives from the contribution made by the merchandiser.

In the case of high pressure merchandising the lower price has mainly been obtained by a mere reduction of the quality of the article, while in the corresponding application of creative merchandising, the lower price has been especially the result of an adaptation of the article to its use, and the introduction of possible modifications and simplifications. It is true that in some cases creative merchandising may also resort to a decrease of the quality of the raw material embodied in the article, but in that case this will be done only after a careful study which has determined that a given article was perhaps of too good a quality for its use, or that this lowering of the quality will have no great effect on the use of the article, whereas in high pressure merchandising this lowering of the quality is used systematically and indiscriminately and is coupled with an attempt to conceal the change, and sometimes even to maintain the former selling price.

The orientation of department stores in the direction of creative merchandising is highly desirable from a number of points of view, among which the following may be stressed.

In no other part of his work does the retailer make a more positive contribution to society than in this activity of creative merchandising. Instead of merely limiting his activity to buying, the merchandiser who enters the field of creative merchandising uses his close contact with the consumer to help the manufacturer to design articles which are better adapted to the needs of the public.

In a period when the right of existence of any form of activity is increasingly questioned and measured according to the positive contribution it makes to the community, and when distributors are frequently attacked and represented as non-productive elements, such an intervention of the retailer in the joint process of production and distribution as that represented by creative merchandising helps to justify the existence of retailing.

On account of its characteristics, its size, and its resources, and the specialized and expert knowledge at its disposal, the department store is in a better position than most other forms of retailing to handle this job of creative merchandising.

Thus S. Schocken has rightly noted that the department stores have a distinct superiority in the matter of creative merchandising, because the variety of the lines of merchandise which they carry and the multiplicity of their experiences and contacts make it possible for them to introduce in some lines of merchandise ideas, innovations or remarkable developments which they have found in other lines. In fact, some of the greatest successes of department stores in the field of creative merchandising have been in transmitting to a specific line of production experiences noted in other lines of goods[9]. Viewed in this way even the widely dissimilar categories of articles carried by department stores throw light on each other.

Furthermore the growing competition of other forms of distribution, as well as the competition within the department store field itself, stressed the necessity for the store to stock non-identical and non-comparable articles.

Here also creative merchandising represents the answer, as one of its main applications consists precisely in taking an article out of the general group, in giving to it distinctive features, modifying or improving it, so as to give to this product individuality and make of it an item exclusive to the store.

Once the importance of this question of creative merchandising, which deserves to be considered as a question of first priority, is recognized, it would of course be necessary to devise the material means necessary to carry it out.

It is probable that the present buyer has neither the time

[9] S. Schocken: "Zwischen Produktion und Konsum. Vier Vorträge über den gegenwärtigen Stand und die Aufgaben des Grosseinzelhandels", Berlin 1931, p. 35.

nor the resources to devote the necessary time and attention to this aspect of his mission. The development of creative merchandising on a considerable scale may thus necessitate some changes or additions in the organization of the firm. The principle of the separation of buying and selling may for instance be adopted, mainly with a view to ensuring that the buyer can devote more time to creative merchandising. Or, according to the suggestion of Wess, one may see the creation of a bureau of design and creative merchandising, placed under the authority of the merchandise manager, and especially entrusted with the job of developing creative merchandising or of helping the buyers in this work.

Whatever the organizational form taken, one may well argue that the development of creative merchandising will be a necessity in the future.

For years past we have seen the other forms of retailing adapt to their needs the innovations and strong points of department stores. We are now in a new era in which it behoves the department store to adapt to its own needs some of the strong features of the newest forms of retailing, as represented by the unit price stores and the chains. Creative merchandising is without any doubt one of the lessons which can be drawn from them. But instead of concentrating, as do the unit price stores, mainly on a single aspect of creative merchandising, namely the modification and simplification of the article in order to offer at lower prices what was hitherto only available at higher prices, the department store must profit from that commercial ubiquity which is one of its greatest assets, and exploit all the different forms of creative merchandising.

In the face of growing competition, department stores will find it advantageous to use the resources of their elaborate merchandise organization for creating new products to fill both old and new wants and for developing changes in old products to make them conform to changes in consumer demand.

Scientific quality control and testing

Scientific quality control and testing is certain to find increasing application in retailing. It is, indeed, surprising that whilst in industry the application of scientific quality control and testing has preceded the application of scientific management, in retailing this sequence has been reversed.

But the trend towards the scientific testing of merchandise is inescapable. The very progress of the textile industry— as in the development of synthetic materials and of improved finishing processes, and the frequent marriages of natural and synthetic fibres—has made the introduction of scientific testing more necessary. It is well-known, for example, that textile products can now be made to appear much better than they really are.

And besides the basic tests referring to the identification of the fabrics and their fibre contents, there is also a wide range of other tests referring to the physical and other properties of the materials, making it possible to compare the merchandise coming from different sources.

One of the advantages of department stores over the traditional forms of retailing has always been that they have been the first to apply more scientific principles. True to their tradition they should also be the first to introduce and profit by scientific quality control and testing.

Some of their newest competitors, especially the unit price stores and the specialty chains, will be able, on account of their more limited assortment and the scale of their purchases, to apply more economically and more completely the advantages of scientific quality control and testing. But this fact makes it even more imperative for the department stores to enter this field, perhaps on a co-operative basis.

National brands and fixed resale prices

We have already pointed out that the growth of national brands and of the practice of resale price maintenance (uniform resale prices fixed by the manufacturers) has helped to reinforce the relative position of the small independent retailer. As is known, the small independent retailer sells mainly convenience merchandise and depends on location rather than on lower prices or exclusivity of the merchandise as a main sales appeal. He has therefore been upheld by the growth of nationally advertised brands and of the principle of fixed resale prices, for the former makes selling easier, while the latter makes profits surer and competition less keen. On the other hand, the development of a variety of well-known and largely diffused articles, strongly supported by national advertising campaigns, and perforce offered at the same price as the remainder of the trade, means for department stores a loss or restriction of these possibilities of differential mark-up which they so often use to attract the public, and is therefore unwelcome.

Another, perhaps even more important characteristic of the national brands is that by the development of these brands and the corresponding national advertising campaigns to push them, manufacturers have established such a firm demand for their products on the part of the consumer that they consider themselves much more independent in relation to retailers.

In fact, the development of national brands supported by advertising on a large scale has served to reduce the scope of the functions of retail distribution. Thus a proportion of the customers come to the store already sold on a particular article—and this reduces the scope of salesmanship. In the same way well-known brands sustained by publicity produce a degree of acceptance which reduces the liberty of action of merchandising.

Under these conditions one understands the dislike with which the modern forms of distribution have watched the expansion of national brands and of fixed resale prices. And this so much the more as national brands and resale price maintenance have made, during the last decades, continuous progress.

This movement is likely to continue. We have thus to consider its ultimate bearing on the relative position of the department stores. In trying to pry into the future, we are inclined to think that we may one day witness a change in the position and opinion of those department stores operated as single stores in relation to these questions.

One must first note that the experience of the past tends to show that national brands and fixed resale prices do not seem to be very suitable for articles with a large style and fashion factor (which will always dominate the assortment of department stores).

There is another more important fact, which may incline department stores to see this question of national brands and fixed resale prices in a new light. In the years to come the most dangerous competition for department stores will come not from the small shopkeepers so much as from the new forms of retailing. The main disadvantage of the department store in relation to chain stores and unit price stores, and perhaps one day even in relation to some small shops grouped into voluntary chains, resides in the fact that it will not be able to muster as great a concentration of buying power on specific lines of merchandise as these forms of distribution and will thus be at a disadvantage as regards purchase prices.

Manufacturers distributing national brands tend to gain a greater hold on the customer and a greater independence in relation to retailers, and to standardize their selling prices, not only to the public, but to retailers also.

Under these conditions one cannot wholly rule out the possibility that one day the department stores (assuming of course that the new forms of retailing represented by the unit price stores and the chain stores are not prevented by artificial stipulations from reaching their full and, one may say, legitimate expansion) may welcome the development of national brands and fixed resale prices as stabilizing factors in their contest with these new forms of retailing, in the same way as the small shopkeepers welcome them today in their fight against department stores.

Fashion and style

It is to be expected that, as in the last decades, the fashion and style factor will continue to increase in importance. Instead of influencing mainly, as of old, the lives of the well-to-do, it will more and more dominate the life of the masses.

The importance of the fashion and style factor is the direct result of the development of the concept of obsolescence. To increase or maintain their sales volumes, merchants and industrialists have developed the concept of obsolescence (which means 'being out-of-date') and have thus tried to replace wear by obsolescence. In itself this concept is fairly old, and it is precisely this idea of obsolescence that has always characterized certain articles, as for example ladies'· and even, in the past, men's garments. But the distinctive feature of these last decades has been to emphasize this conception and to extend it to a great number of new articles. Leaving aside the typical example of the automobile where the 'new' model is bought long before the 'old' is worn out, one may note a great number of articles in the assortment of the department store where an element of style or fashion has been introduced, precisely in order to profit by the obsolescence factor. A typical example is offered by women's shoes, which in the course of the last decades have been converted from staples to short-lived fashion merchandise, with plain black shoes losing their former dominating position. One can mention a great number of articles in which the element of obsolescence and of style and fashion has been introduced by the use of colour, changes of shape or design, new materials, etc.

This movement has thus not only increased the requirements of the public as regards fashion and style in the strictly fashion departments such as ladies' outer garments and millinery, but has also introduced the style and fashion factor in such departments as linens, dress goods, hosiery, etc., where it formerly played only a secondary rôle. This style and fashion factor tends steadily to invade new fields. Even for articles like furniture, kitchen utensils, radios—not to speak of automobiles—fashion, i.e., obsolescence, has replaced wear and tear as the main motive for the purchase of a new item.

Supported by sales promotion, obsolescence has been developed into a psychological pressure on the customer and has become an art of increasing consumer demand artificially.

Everything points to the fact that this movement is likely to continue and to be accelerated in the future. The growing tendency of Europe to look to America for inspiration is already an assurance of such an accelerated trend, as American business is precisely the one which uses most widely this means of fighting against market saturation. As stated recently by C. Wright Mills: "The whole of fashion, not only in clothing, automobiles and furniture, but in virtually all commodities is deliberately managed to the end of greater sales volume . . . U.S. society has in crucial aspects become a continuous fashion show"[10].

This evolution may reinforce the position of department stores, first by helping to increase retail sales, but mainly because the department stores, on account of their very characteristics, have revealed themselves to be in a better position than any other form of retailing for the study, anticipation, and promotion of fashions. By their appreciable unit size and the multiplicity of the lines of merchandise carried, by their wide contact with many markets, by their organization and background, department stores seem to be at a distinct advantage in the forecasting, launching and popularization of fashions. They have, furthermore, the chance, which they may increasingly exploit in the future, of employing skilled help in forecasting style. In fact, no other form of retailing is or can be so well equipped as the department store to follow and to turn to useful account the varying needs, fashions and fancies of the day.

It is true that the increase of the fashion factor will theoretically entail an increase in the operating expenses of department stores, since the handling of fashion articles involves greater risks and greater merchandising and selling expenses than the handling of staple goods. But it is probable that the development of modern methods of merchandising (as regards, for example, the study of consumer demand, the planning of the assortment and the control of the stock) and even of selling (for example in the direction of the classification and systematic display of the assortment) may help to keep these increased costs within reasonable limits.

The growing importance of the fashion and style factors may be working in favour of the department store and will

---

[10] C. Wright Mills: "White Collar—The American Middle Classes," New York 1951, p. 164.

reinforce its position, provided that the department store adapts its method of operation to this trend.

The consequence of this evolution must be a continuation and a reinforcement of the tendency to keep smaller inventories, to adopt hand-to-mouth buying methods, and to attach in the rating of the different suppliers a greater importance than formerly to the factor of rapid delivery.

Further, the development of modern methods of stock analysis and stock control, such as unit control records with their measurement of the needs of the public, and the periodic stock reviews with a marking and special treatment of old age merchandise, have already in the past been a direct outcome of the growth of the fashion factor. One foresees that their applications will become increasingly numerous in the future, concurrently with the continued development of this factor.

A continuation of the practice of establishing buying offices in the supply markets is equally likely to follow, since this practice is also the result of the development of the fashion and style factor which makes it necessary to have first-hand information more easily available, to buy more rapidly and especially more frequently smaller lots of the newest offerings.

Department stores have an advantage to gain in sponsoring the development of the fashion and style factor, because such a trend reinforces their position in relation to the smaller retailer or the new forms of distribution. As regards the latter (unit price stores and chain stores) it is important for the department store to see that the fashion trends take the form of changing waves of relatively short duration, so as to prevent these new forms of retail distribution, which are very dependent on the limiting factor 'time', from bringing into play their assets of mass purchase and standardization; for these can come into action only if a given fashion lasts a considerable time. In this respect, a continuation of the trend of these last decades with a constant acceleration of the speed with which styles and fashion change, will be favourable to department stores.

Mark-downs

While part of the mark-downs represent unavoidable changes in general conditions and in public demand, and also one of the characteristics of department store operation, namely the offering of new merchandise at relatively higher prices with a subsequent lowering of the mark-up, another portion of the mark-downs is due to inefficient buying, ineffective merchandise planning, faulty merchandise control, etc. In fact, many mark-downs are taken on merchandise which should never have been bought or on merchandise overbought in quantity.

It is from this latter standpoint that the evolution of the rate of mark-downs of a store, over a number of years, may be considered as a yardstick of the efficiency of its merchandising organization.

The average rate of mark-downs of department stores was in the United States around eight per cent. of the sales of the whole store in 1930 (and from 15 to 20 per cent. in the women's ready-to-wear division). Experts like Mazur and Wess stated at that time that the ideal mark-down figure ought to lie around five per cent.

During the last decade preceding the second world war decisive steps were taken in this direction. By a better selection of the articles bought, the introduction of modern methods of assortment planning and stock control, American department stores were able to improve their mark-down figures to a mere six/seven per cent.

It is on this problem of mark-down reduction by better assortment planning and stock control that American department stores concentrated most of their efforts during the period 1930-1940. Thanks to the reduction of the rate of mark-down, to better merchandising and stock control, they were able in 1938 to reach the profits of 1929, in spite of a smaller volume of sales and slightly higher expenses.

A similar concentration of effort on the reduction of the rate of mark-downs may represent a very promising approach for those European department stores which to date do not excel in this direction.

The mere fact that we are going to experience during the decades to come an increase in the importance of the fashion and style factor, and consequently of the potential danger of greater mark-downs, will itself help to stress the desirability of this approach. A number of authorities on department store problems have stated, when looking at the problem of department store operation improvement as a whole, that mark-downs represent in their view one of the most promising single avenues of study.

It is, however, necessary to record that in some of our stores that approach could not work, because there are a number of European department stores where the mark-down rate is not too high but, on the contrary, too low. Such exaggeratedly low figures often reflect an abnormal composition of the trade with a preponderance of staple goods, and also too great a uniformity of mark-up (in relation to time), without the use of this current department store practice of showing style merchandise for a short time at relatively high price, with a subsequent mark-down to dispose rapidly of the remaining stock.

One may suggest that stores of the latter category are operated under conditions which will make them an easy prey to the normal development of the newer forms of distribution (unit price stores and specialty chains) and that they require a change of methods and character which, while increasing their rate of mark-down, will make of them what a department store ought to be, namely a "magasin de nouveautés".

Service departments and customer services

We have seen, in reviewing the history of the department store, how the continuous development of service departments and customer services has been used as a powerful element of customer attraction.

This use of the service element by the department store is sound, as it corresponds to one of the major principles of commercial strategy which consists of playing on one's own strong points. By the very nature of its form of business, by virtue of its greater average unit size and the existence of so many different selling departments in the same store, the department store is in a position to give to its service departments and customer services an extension in number and scope which is beyond the reach of any other form of retailing.

In following this trend the department store was developing in a direction where it was in a position to perform a major job of providing customer convenience more economically than any other form of distribution, and it is only natural that it should fully exploit this advantage.

During a fairly long period this development represented a reinforcement of the position of department stores and an increase of their power of public attraction. But a stage has gradually been reached where service departments and customer services have become a major tool in the fierce competition for volume between department stores. A real race, which we have already compared to a race of armaments, has taken place among the department stores in respect of the number of services granted to customers and the liberality shown in interpreting their rules of operation. A complicated and expensive superstructure of customer services has thus gradually been built. It is perhaps particularly pronounced in the American and Parisian stores, but represents nevertheless a general trend.

By competing in the services offered department stores have even in many cases gone beyond the actual requirements of the customers. The result of this evolution has been an increase in the cost of operation and in the prices of department stores to a point where they were out of proportion to the value of the service for the average customer.

To this day there has been no investigation to determine the total and real cost represented by all these service departments and customer services. If this total cost were established it would reach an amount appreciably higher than the total publicity expenses. It represents today one of the causes of the higher cost of distribution of department stores; most of these services are absent or at least are offered to a much more limited extent in other lines of retailing.

The first step to be taken to cope with this problem consists in determining the total cost represented by the service departments and the customer services. Such a factual inquiry will yield results which may upset many accepted ideas. It will probably reveal that the total expenses of service departments and customer services represent from five to eight per cent. of the sales.

To deal quantitatively with only two of these items, we may record that it has been calculated that in the average American department store, with its rate of returns of 10 per cent., the returns practice involves for the store a cost representing some one per cent. of sales[11]. This last figure may seem very high; but it has been calculated with considerable accuracy, and one must remember that some returns made in connection with charge sales are expensive transactions, involving the following operations: sale, charge, delivery, return, collection and subsequent credit and exchange. As regards the charge account business, its extra cost has been estimated by a careful computation to represent about three per cent. of the sales concerned[12]. This figure is substantial and means that in a department store where the charge account business represents half the turnover, the extra cost of charge account business is about 1.5 per cent. of the total sales.

Thus in the typical American store merely two of these service elements, the returns and the charge accounts, involve extra costs which represent 2.5 per cent. of the sales. It is against the background of such data that the problem must be considered.

Once it is realized that the total cost of the service departments and customer services represents an amount about equal to the cost of the selling service proper, the issue will fall into its proper perspective.

While appreciating the sales promotional significance of the service to customers factor, one may argue that the extent of services granted must, in the future, mainly be determined from the point of view of the competition between the department stores, considered as a whole, and other forms of distribution, and not, as heretofore, mainly from the point of view of the competition of department stores between themselves. It is a question of

[11] See J. Lowrie: "The Cost of Handling Merchandise Returns", Columbus 1929.

[12] See B. Emmet: "Department Stores", Stanford 1930, p. 121.

finding the right relationship and of suppressing costly exaggerations.

Sales promotion

The problem of the sales promotion function offers a great similarity to that of service departments and customer services.

Here also we have a factor which the department stores were bound to use because the very nature of their form of enterprise put them in a better position than the other forms of distribution to utilize it effectively.

This arises first from the fact that the money spent upon advertising is more effective, out of all proportion, as the scale of expenditure increases. The expenditure of £100,000 on advertising by a single firm has far more effect than a hundred publicity budgets of £1,000 each. The greater average unit size of department stores has also enabled them to have on their payroll qualified specialists working full time on their advertising and display. Finally the combination of many merchandise groups in the same firm makes it possible to promote different articles at the same time with corresponding possibilities of savings by combination, or to use the opportunities of mutual support offered by the interplay of the various merchandise lines. Customers attracted by the advertising of one department will also buy in others. A single insertion may contain descriptions of merchandise offered in several departments. Moreover, media of advertising can be used which are impossible for smaller stores, on account of their limited clientele or of the limited area from which they draw trade.

As is known, sales promotion, especially in the form of advertising, is one of the factors which has made possible the great development of department stores. It has conferred on this form of distribution one of its most distinctive features and has contributed towards its success.

We have already quoted the severe but probably just judgment of Nystrom, who stated that one of the characteristics of the operation of department stores, when compared with for example specialty stores, resided in the fact that they replaced skilled salesmanship by skilled advertising.

However, with time, this element of success has tended in some countries (for instance America) to become an element of weakness because the advertising expenses have continuously reached higher levels, whilst the pulling power of these advertising expenses has tended to become smaller.

Many factors have contributed towards this situation. One must first consider that the cost of advertising has had a tendency to increase, on account of the greater use of advertising, the wider circulation of the newspapers and the rise in the standard of advertising brought about by its technical progress.

Further, since the use of advertising is usually coupled with the use of sales promotional mark-downs, one may note that the actual expenses of advertising are actually much higher than those reflected by the corresponding items of the standard classification of expenses. Such an inclusion would show that the total sales promotion expenses represent between five and eight per cent. of the sales.

The growing volume of advertising has also served to dissipate the attention of readers over a great number of insertions, and has thus decreased the pulling power of advertising.

But the main cause of this evolution has probably been the use of advertising as one of the major weapons of department stores in their competition within the department store field itself. One has witnessed, for example in America, exaggerations reminiscent of the excesses we have already noted as regards customer services, and which we have compared to a kind of armaments race.

One must also note the growing use or misuse of this medium of sales promotion under a perverted form which we have called high pressure sales promotion, for imposing on the customer, by sheer psychological pressure, the purchase of articles which she did not desire, and which in many cases she could not afford to buy.

In order to straighten out this situation there are perhaps two main approaches. First, it is of vital importance for department stores to be able to establish a relationship between the cost of advertising and its results. Some methods of advertising response control have already been developed. They deserve to be used and amplified so as to give to the application of advertising a more quantitative character than heretofore and thus reduce the wastes resulting from a misdirected effort. The aim of these investigations must be a suppression of the present arbitrary use of the different sales promotion media. Secondly, the tendency of department stores to compete with each other on volume of advertising done (as they already compete on price, style, services, etc.) ought to be brought within reasonable limits by mutual agreement: as with the amount of service granted, the amount of advertising done by department stores ought to be governed by the interest of the department store line as a whole, rather than by the desire to engage in internecine strife by means of advertising volume.

There is no doubt that the department store derives much benefit from extensive advertising which seems more effective in the hands of department stores than in those of any other form of retail distribution. But there again, we must keep a sense of proportion. The use of advertising must serve a purpose and not degenerate into a weapon of ruthless competition between department stores, for the ultimate result of such practices is an exaggerated use of advertising by all department stores in a market which has reached its saturation point, with a corresponding increase in the cost of distribution of this form of retailing.

Sales promotion events

In themselves sales promotion events have their legitimate place in the operation of department stores. When they have been suppressed by legislative stipulation, as in Germany under the Third Reich, we have seen the department stores feel the need to find substitutes in the form of timely concentrations of all the sales promotion media on given merchandise groups.

But here again it is not the sales promotion events as such which are involved, but the exaggeration in their number and scope. This abuse has helped create the deplorable impression that the department stores have two different and parallel businesses, the regular price business and the special price business. This has induced in many customers the habit of waiting for special offerings. The generalization of sales promotional events is also responsible for the breaking down of the loyalty of customers to a given store and for creating a special category of customers who are mere sales events followers and bargain hunters.

Nothing illustrates better the abuse which the practice of sales promotion events has become than their effect on the employment of the personnel. Besides fulfilling the aim of clearing old merchandise, sales events were originally devised with the idea of ensuring to the store a greater continuity of employment, by reviving the sales during the dullest periods. Now, on the contrary, sales events exercise rather the opposite effect: they involve periods when the staff of the enterprise is hastily increased by additional and untrained help, to be followed by periods in which, even after the discharge of these extra employees, the normal staff is not fully employed.

Here again the first step to an improvement of the situation is the possession of facts. Quantitative data must be collected on the scope and extent of the sales promotion events, such as on the percentage of yearly sales made in sales events, the percentage of the total sales promotion budget spent on sales events, the determination of the sales increases over normal due to sales events, the determination of the percentage of the total sales of each event made on marked-down articles, comparisons between the mark-up of the regular and special price articles sold during the events, etc.

This information could be completed by the establishment of the profit and loss statement of some sales promotional events. Such a statement would compare the additional sales obtained by the event to the total expenses that it has caused. These expenses include not only the additional expenses directly caused by the event (and one must not forget to include among them such indirect items as the cost of the increase in the rate of returns after the event), but also the mark-up sacrifices made for the event and the anticipated mark-downs on overbought merchandise.

One may assume that the collection of such data may be the starting point for a sounder use of sales promotion events.

As an element of normal sales promotion (and one may add of normal merchandising as regards the clearance sales) sales promotion events have undoubtedly their place in the operation of department stores. But when used systematically as a main tool in the fight against other department stores and in the task of concealing the high cost of distribution of department stores, they largely defeat their own purpose.

Extended sales promotion budget

It would also be very advisable to create, beside the usual sales promotion budget which covers advertising and display expenses, an extended sales promotion budget which would include all the expenses or sacrifices involved in the promotion of sales.

This extended sales promotion budget would include, besides the advertising and display expenses, the sales promotional mark-downs (with the exception of the clearance mark-downs), the losses or expenses caused by the service departments and customer services, and perhaps also the discounts granted to customers.

Such a united approach would allow the general management to adjust the rival claims of various functions upon the sums spent in sales promotion and to direct the sales promotion efforts and expenses, considered in their broadest sense, from a wider angle.

Unlike the sales promotion budget, the extended sales promotion budget would not be placed under the exclusive authority of the sales promotion manager, because any decision referring to an increase or decrease of the sums spent on sales promotional mark-downs or service departments and customer services directly affects other functions.

But such an instrument is of inestimable value when the general management is considering the policies of the firm as a whole, as it will offer a comprehensive picture of all the efforts made with a view to maintaining or increasing the sales, and will thus provide the possibility of welding these efforts into a cohesive whole. These different items, which have hitherto been treated in watertight compartments, are in reality closely interlinked. The question of sales promotion is a whole, and its parts are interdependent. Unless it is viewed as a whole there will be confusion of thought and policy. The existence of that extended sales promotion budget makes it possible to bring each of these items into a correct perspective, to examine the interplay of these factors, to mobilize the resources devoted to sales promotion in the directions which are considered the most effective, as well as to carry out a series of experiments in order to identify the most effective means of sales promotion.

The eventual result of such an extended sales promotion budget may well be an effective contribution towards solving this problem of the reduction of the total sales promotion expenses of a department store by a more rational apportionment and concentration of these expenses in the most effective directions, a problem whose solution we have already mentioned as one of the needs of the future.

Equal treatment of all customers

The equal treatment of all customers has been one of the superior virtues and elements of attraction of department stores since their creation. This equal treatment has been embodied in the suppression of bargaining, the practice of offering only merchandise with fixed and marked prices. Even the less intimate contact between the department store staff and the customers (as compared, for example, with the conditions existing in the specialty stores) has been, from this point of view, an asset for the department store, as it has suppressed or reduced discrimination in favour of certain customers.

It is arguable that department stores have retained these characteristics. But some of the developments of department store operation during the last decades, especially the extension of services and the greater use of high pressure sales promotion, have served to create new discriminations. Under their influence the principle of the equal treatment of all customers has tended to fade away. Thus one may think that in the modern department store the 'cash' customer subsidises the 'charge account' customer, the 'take' customer the 'send' customer, and the 'regular price' customer the 'reduced offer' customer.

There is here, without any doubt, a situation fraught with dangers, and this so much the more as the other forms of retailing, which are usually free from the exaggerated use of service to customers and high pressure sales promotion, are in a position to ensure to their clientele a more equal treatment in respect of the points listed.

The solution of this difficult question, at least as regards the discrimination between the regular price and the reduced offer customers, probably lies in a reduction of the number and scope of those special offers which are themselves tied up with the high pressure sales promotion methods whose advisability we have already questioned.

As regards the differential treatment between cash and charge account customers, or take and send customers, a possible solution would consist in charging to charge account and send customers a proportion of the extra cost which this form of transaction implies. Such measures could, of course, only be taken within the frame of a general collective agreement between the department stores of a given town, and would have to be explained by a campaign of propaganda.

Modern forms of selling

In spite of the fact that we foreshadow the reinforcement of the position of the department stores by a development of their own resources rather than by an imitation of the features of the new forms of distribution, we do not see why the department stores should not adopt and adapt to their own needs some of the strong points of these enterprises.

The method of selling of the unit price stores, which we have called a semi-self-service selling method, where the merchandise is arranged and classified in open displays and where the customers perform their own selection and sometimes even the fitting, with a minimum of assistance from the sales people, is one of them. It is by means of this method of semi-self-service selling that unit price stores achieve an average number of daily transactions per sales assistant of some 200-220.

Besides giving to the merchandise a better chance to sell itself, semi-self-service selling increases the productivity of the sales assistant by suppressing part of his work (getting out the merchandise for presentation and later putting it again in place), by transferring another portion of his work to the customer (who however does not mind it, but rather the contrary) and by enabling the sales assistant to concentrate on the only portions of his job where his intervention is really indispensable, namely the last steps of the transaction. Further, semi-self-service selling speeds up the transaction from the point of view of the customer.

It can be contended, in fact, that in a way semi-self-service selling represents a division of the sales transaction which brings to distribution some of the advantages that division of labour has brought to manufacturing.

A partial application of this system of semi-self-service selling can take place in department stores for a number of departments (mainly toilet requisites, haberdashery, hardware, stationery, some ladies' dress accessories, some underwear, etc.) by the adoption of classified open display for part of the assortment.

More generally one must sponsor an increased use of the so-called assortment system of display, the use of displays which present a complete range of samples of the different styles and prices stocked, so that customers can make their selection with little or no aid from the salespeople. That is to say, instead of displaying (as is usually the case nowadays) a handkerchief or a piece of underwear carefully draped against a perfume bottle or a glove with the fingers pointed upward on some form, one would display all the types of gloves, all the lengths or colours of hosiery, many of the types of underwear, thus giving to the customers a chance of making their own selection[13].

While the combined mass and assortment display, in the same way as in the unit price stores, with the customer

---

[13] See Kenneth Collins: "The Trend toward Self-Service", Journal of Retailing, December 1940.

actually picking out the article from the display, is, in the case of the department store only possible in a few departments, there are wide possibilities for other types of assortment display. An example is the complete sample assortment, a display of all styles, sizes and colours stocked, so that the customers can make undirected selections and then call on the assistant to get a duplicate of the desired article from the stock. Another type of display is the so-called complete style assortment with a display of all styles carried, but not of the colours and sizes, so that the customer can make a primary selection but must depend on the assistance of a sales person before making the final choice.

The extension of this system of semi-self-service selling to ready-to-wear may even be considered in some cases. There exist dress departments with each section devoted to dresses of a unit price and with, within each section, the stock clearly divided according to size, and so presented that there is direct access of the clientele to the stock.

There are nowadays clothing stores run along these lines, with the customer selecting her garment, trying it on, and taking it to the cashier and wrapping desk. The conversion of some other departments and sections along lines similar to those of the self-service grocery stores is also taking place.

This trend toward semi-self-service and even full self-service selling corresponds to the desires of the public and to the requirements of efficiency. As noted by Kenneth Collins, a growing number of customers prefer to make their own undirected selection: they wish ample freedom to examine and compare without feeling that somebody else is trying to force or speed up a decision.

Further, the usual method of selling articles hidden behind fixtures and under counters is not efficient. It obliges the sales assistant to pull out quantities of stock from shelves, drawers and cabinets, to stand about while the customer meditates, and laboriously to put the goods back again after a choice has been made.

Finally one may consider that telephone selling represents one of the directions along which department stores ought to develop, in accordance with the principle of expansion along those paths where department stores, by virtue of their very characteristics, have the advantage over the remainder of the retail trade. The advantage enjoyed by the department store in the direction of telephone selling resides first of all in the fact that the great variety of merchandise lines allows the customer to make several purchases through one telephone call. Another lies in the fact that department stores are the form of distribution which uses advertising to the largest extent. They can thus encourage the stay-at-home customers to order by telephone the merchandise which they have seen advertised in the newspaper, through direct mail advertising and otherwise.

There is no doubt that the increasing traffic congestion in the central shopping section of the great towns will encourage telephone selling of staple goods. We have, moreover, already pointed out that progress in the technique of long-distance calls may result in an increase in the portion of the clientele of metropolitan department stores living in other parts of the country and ordering by telephone.

Selling departments

From the origin of department store history the departments selling piece goods and ladies' outer garments have represented the backbone of these establishments. The customers attracted by these merchandise groups were in a way the main customers and bought readily in several other selling departments of the store, while the converse is less true. In fact, the reputations of most department stores have been largely based on the success of these departments.

As regards the piece goods departments, the trend towards buying more and more ready-to-wear has perhaps contributed to a decrease in the relative importance of this group of merchandise, an evolution which has been on the whole detrimental to the interests of department stores, but in the face of which the stores are powerless.

A transformation which offers even greater dangers, and for which certain department stores are directly responsible, resides in the fact that some of them have let the basic departments represented by ladies' outer garments become weak and non-competitive.

The causes of such deterioration, one may even say degeneration, are numerous. In some cases it is the development of a house product which has revealed itself incapable of competing with the products from outside suppliers. The growth of department stores along lines far afield from their original business has also helped to draw the attention of the management away from the ladies' dress departments, these, seen out of true perspective, having been treated like any other department, whereas they are in fact the basic departments of a store.

Perhaps one of the most urgent needs of any department store where such a situation exists is to correct it by an investigation of the conditions prevailing in the department and the taking of the necessary measures.

It may also be estimated that, on account of the paramount importance of the ladies' dress department, it is advisable to operate for this department a system of statistical control of the merchandise (unit control), analyzing the sales and the stock by segregating them by classes, price lines, sizes, age, colours, manufacturers, etc. Even if unit control is not used in the other selling departments of the store, its utilization for this particular merchandise line is fully justified by the prominence of the corresponding selling department.

Another aspect of the question of the operation of selling departments refers to the treatment of those selling departments which reveal themselves as losing departments not in one department store, but in the whole department store field.

In cases where these selling departments represent merchandise groups mainly developed in the department store line and where the competition of the other forms of distribution is not strong, a common decision of the local department stores to increase the mark-up and to reduce some expense items may relatively easily render such departments profitable. But there are other selling departments which are not profitably operated in department stores and of which other forms of distribution make a more successful job. It is probable that with the development of the unit price store and particularly of the specialty chains, the number of these departments will have a tendency to increase.

One of the future tasks of department stores is to identify, by means of departmental accounting, such selling departments, and to take, if necessary, drastic measures perhaps going as far as the use of new forms of distribution, in order to eliminate these sources of loss. One may, for example, foresee in those merchandise lines where the specialty chains, on account of their central merchandising and mass purchasing, have a great advantage, the development of specialized chains of leased departments. As is known, such organisms with a central buying organization and whose branches are represented by selling departments of a specific line, leased in a number of department stores, are found in America, especially strongly represented in certain merchandise lines such as millinery.

Non-selling departments and the concept of productivity

The proportion of selling to non-selling personnel has, as is known, declined continuously in the course of the history of the department store. This decline has been caused by the growing division of labour, the increase in the number and scope of the services granted to the clientele, the influence of the size factor and the development of the organization of department stores.

While at the beginning of department stores the selling personnel represented 70 per cent. of the total staff, there are now department stores where it represents less than 40 per cent. of the total staff (production workrooms excluded).

This evolution is in itself natural enough and perhaps even inevitable, since it reflects the growing refinement of the means of distribution represented by the department store; but there is evidently a lower limit which cannot be ignored without making of the department store a too complicated and costly form of retailing.

The most direct approach to the solution of this problem, besides the reduction of the service departments and customer services to a reasonable level (a subject already treated) consists of a better control of the operation of non-selling departments by the introduction of operating standards, and of the concept of productivity. As noted by P. J. Reilly, the absence of measuring sticks to determine whether operating performance is really efficient may be considered one of the causes of the consistent increase in the department store expenses.

The expenses of a non-selling department are usually planned, established and controlled on two bases: the absolute expenses of the department and the expenses of the department as a percentage of the total sales of the store. But any study of the actual operation and conditions of operation of non-selling departments will show that these bases are not rational.

First, we must never forget that in a department store the non-selling departments have no control over the volume of their operations. Their load of work depends solely upon the activities of the selling departments.

Secondly, the general concept that the non-selling departments are responsible for maintaining the cost of their operation at certain levels in relation to sales, which is a result of the general habit of department stores of basing expenses and operation upon percentages of net sales, is false in the case of the non-selling departments. A store which has budgeted a certain figure for its total net sales for the coming year may reach this total figure with a change in the distribution of the share of the various lines of merchandise in the total sales, and this may greatly change the load of work placed on some non-selling departments. Moreover, a rise in the price of the merchandise will, in the system of expense control by percentage of sales, automatically increase the budget of the non-selling departments, although their load of work, measured by the number of units of production, will not increase. On the other hand, in a period of declining merchandise prices the budget of the non-selling department, expressed in percentage of sales, will decrease, while the actual load of work may remain the same.

Department stores must do in the years to come for the non-selling departments what they have done in the last decades for the selling departments—develop effective means allowing a check of the performances of these sections, thus making it possible to keep their expenses under control.

The first step in this direction is to choose or develop suitable units for measuring the performance or production of these non-selling departments.

We give below a tentative list of the units of production which may be considered for a number of non-selling departments:

Department	*Units of production or performance*
Accounts payable	number of invoices handled or number of lines posted
Accounts receivable	number of charge transactions posted or number of lines billed
Addressing	number of new plates prepared and number of envelopes printed
Bookkeeping	number of entries made
Buying office	number of orders placed
Collection	number of collections made
Correspondence	number of lines typed
Cost and selling accounting	number of invoices treated
Credit	number of credit applications investigated
Delivery	number of "weighted" deliveries
Duplicating	number of stencils cut and number of copies produced
Employment	number of persons hired, discharged and reclassified
Mailing	number of pieces of mail handled
Marking	number of pieces marked
Order filling	number of order lines
Payroll	number of wage envelopes ("weighted")
Receiving	number of invoices and returns ("weighted") or tonnage handled

Department	Units of production or performance
Sales dissecting	number of sales bills treated
Sign shop	number of signs ("weighted" by size)
Stockrooms	number of stock requisition lines
Statistical:	
punching	number of cards punched
sorting	number of cards sorted
tabulating	number of cards tabulated or number of tabulating machine hours
Traffic	number of routings and of shipping claims
Tube room	number of transactions handled
Warehouse	as for receiving and stockrooms

As noted by P. Laguionie: "Our experience has shown us that the mere study or determination of these units of production is, by itself, a most powerful means of organisation, as you can select them only after a careful study of the operation of a department, which you see then for the first time under a new light, as a machine for producing a given service".

Once these units of production are selected and recorded they may be used to control the productivity of the non-selling departments or of specific sections within the non-selling departments.

A first means of control consists in dividing the expenses of a non-selling department by the number of units produced, with the corresponding determination of a unit cost, the evolution of which will be followed from month to month (after a possible segregation of the influence of the fixed expenses).

However, the modern concept of productivity mainly refers to physical units. According to this concept, it is not the expenses of the department but the number of man-hours worked in that department which is used for the determination of the number of units produced per man-hour worked in each non-selling department.

The introduction of these units of production, of these unit costs or of these standards of production per man-hour, for control of the work of the non-selling departments, will change the outlook of these departments. They will be judged on the basis of their actual achievements, i.e., their volume of production, their production per man-hour, their ability to decrease unit costs, to adapt their expenses to the fluctuations of their volume of production or their production per man-hour.

As stated by S. Bögelund-Jensen, the advantages of the division of labour, on which the department store is based, are lost unless you can continuously measure and control the activities of each of the specialized activities among which the store has been divided.

Store management

The store management function is probably one of the fields of department store operation offering the greatest opportunities for reducing expenses and making direct savings. A review of the Harvard statistics on the operating results of department stores discloses that the expense items over which the store management function has control, and which include, amongst others, occupancy, repairs, services purchased, supplies, delivery, receiving and marking, are those which show the relatively greatest increase between 1920 and 1940.

The store management function has materially added to the cost of distribution of department stores. While some of these store management expenses represent, in fact, the cost of service departments and customer services and require for their reduction a treatment of the service problem as a whole, there is no doubt that a direct approach which consists in detecting the possibilities of savings and of increased efficiency within this function, is equally promising.

Several management consulting engineers, when entrusted with the task of guiding the reorganization of department stores, have deliberately started their job by some aspect of the store management function. They have chosen that approach as the one most likely to produce tangible savings rapidly.

It is a fact that delivery departments seem to represent the most promising field of saving in European department stores. It is interesting to note, when comparing the average expense percentages of European and American department stores, that the functional division "delivery" is the only one where the American figures (as a percentage of sales) are consistently and appreciably lower than the corresponding rates for European stores[14].

Personnel

In accordance with the principle which we have followed in the course of this investigation, we do not intend to treat here the multitude of problems which refer to the personnel function of a department store, but only to present what we consider as the broader issues relating to the question.

First one may suggest that the introduction of sounder personnel policies and of a more liberal outlook in employer-employee relations is a necessity, that "humanizing" of personnel relations is essential for the successful operation of any enterprise. Chief executives will have to think in terms of employee satisfaction and happiness as much as in terms of returns on investment[15].

The personnel problem will, however, also present itself under other aspects.

From its very origin the department store was partly based, thanks to the possibilities of organization, division of labour and of the principle of delegation of skill, on the use of a personnel which was on the whole of a lower class, but also more economical, than that of the specialty stores. That situation has continued for years without too much inconvenience, the department stores using, as noted by Nystrom, skilled advertising as a substitute for skilled salesmanship.

However, in the course of the last decades a change in the outlook of department stores in relation to the personnel problem has taken place. They have created extensive

---

[14] See P. Reilly: "A Lesson in Operation from England", Bulletin of the N.R.D.G.A., October 1935, p. 20.

[15] A. Goudsmit: Presidential Address to the International Association of Department Stores, Paris, 6th November, 1947

employment and training departments with a view to selecting better human material and to ensuring better qualified personnel, especially in the sales force.

These efforts to raise the quality of the personnel, by training, have probably been due to the following reasons. In the period of greater competition which has characterized these last decades, department store executives have gradually woken up to the fact that one of the weaknesses of their form of business, when compared with specialty stores, lay in the loss of sales or (even more important) in the loss of patronage due to poor salesmanship. Any serious comparative audit would show that one of the greatest liabilities of department stores resides in the indifference of the staff, a situation which derives from the size of the department store, the conditions of work, and the salary level. It is true that the other competitors of department stores, such as chain stores and unit price stores, have a sales force even weaker than that of the department stores. But in these forms of retailing which cater largely for convenience goods, the personality of the sales assistant is not so much a requisite as in the department store which caters for shopping goods. Further, the growing importance of the fashion factor in the articles forming the assortment of department stores, as well as the tendency of some department stores to trade up in order to leave the field occupied by unit price stores and specialty chains and to meet their growing expenses by higher average transactions, would be sufficient in itself to warrant the growing efforts of department stores to train and instruct their sales force. Finally the desire (or necessity) to use, in the face of strong competition, high pressure selling methods, has perhaps also been not unrelated to these efforts.

Under such conditions the sums spent on the training of the personnel, even if they contribute to increase the expenses, are doubtless justified. One must also consider the fact that no other form of distribution, not even the chain store or specialty chain, is in a position to perform that work of training so effectively and economically as the department store. In fact, no other form of retailing is performing that work on such an extensive scale.

But unfortunately the benefits accruing to the department stores from this effort are not as great as could be expected, mainly because of the excessive rate of labour turnover.

Department stores should realize that they cannot gain full advantage from their expensive training schemes if they do not reduce their exaggerated labour turnover, for the latter means that the majority of the sales assistants they train are lost to them after a relatively short period of employment.

It must also be borne in mind that the general trend of the department stores, considered as a whole, to trade up reinforces the importance of this greater stability in personnel. As stated by Henry Smith, "In some branches of retailing the cost of labour turnover is very high. Not only do assistants have to be trained in the technique of the trade, but in the policy of the firm; moreover, personal contact with customers places a very high value upon the personality of the salesman. For example, in the high-class furniture trade, the retailer will be very reluctant indeed to alter his staff. At the other extreme, however, in the case of Woolworth's, where the salesman is a nonentity behind the counter, neither informing nor influencing the consumer, but merely engaged in collecting money and preventing petty larceny, the position is entirely different. Here the cost of labour turnover is relatively slight"[16].

Finally there is another important facet of the personnel problem, the question of remuneration, which is closely related to the aforementioned questions of the quality and stability of the staff.

Department store operation has until these very last decades largely been based on cheap, unskilled labour. This has been made possible partly by the division of labour and the character of operation of department stores, and partly by the fact that a large part of their staff was composed of young women employees who lived at home or were partly supported by parents. Department stores have thus profited by relatively low wages—at the cost, it is

---

[16] H. Smith: "Retail Distribution", London 1937, p. 26.

true, of relatively low qualitative and quantitative performance.

It seems certain that by the mere force of circumstances department stores will be obliged in the years to come to abandon this attitude. One must first take into consideration the growing strength of the trade unions and the inevitable spread of professional organization to department store personnel.

One must also reckon with the fact that our modern way of life entails a gradual disappearance of the type of women who were able to live on a relatively small wage because they were supported by their family. We are drifting towards a society where the great majority of people will be self-supporting.

As regards the remuneration of the personnel, perhaps the only way the department store can avoid the consequences, on their operating figures, of higher levels of remuneration, is for them to prepare themselves to set and obtain higher standards of performance from their staff.

This increase in performance must be both qualitative and quantitative. From the point of view of the qualitative increase of the performances it is the training department which must take the main share in the realization of this aim. As regards the increase of the quantitative performance, this is mainly the field of work of the research department. It must study, devise and introduce the methods and standards of performance necessary to measure, increase and control the productivity of the staff.

Utilization of the personnel

One of the familiar drawbacks of the retail trade is the fact that the activity of the staff, especially of the selling staff, is directly dependent on the flow of customers: While a manufacturing firm can stock both materials and labour (the latter by producing for stock), retailing can only stock merchandise but not labour.

Because of the wide seasonal, daily and hourly fluctuations of the flow of customers, the utilization of the personnel is incomplete and translates itself into the existence of a considerable proportion of idle time. The bearing of this fact on the cost of distribution is obvious.

But while this disadvantage is felt by the whole retail trade, one may say that the department store, on account of its very principle of departmentalization, is even more subjected to it than most other forms of retailing. This principle of departmentalization, whilst it brings efficiency by virtue of the qualifications of the employees, also causes waste. Thus in a departmentalized store there may be slack times in the work of some departments or employees, whereas the employees of a smaller shop operated as a single unit, are more easily used, when there are slack times in the selling activity, to perform other duties. A typical example is the delivery boy of a small store who may help in selling in rush hours[17].

The question of the utilization of the personnel deserves to be treated here from a double point of view. First because it is evident that a more complete and steady utilization of the personnel will manifest itself in a reduction of the cost of distribution, one of the main problems of retailing in general, but of department stores in particular.

A second argument of equal importance lies in the fact that, as any investigation will show, department stores are by their size and their characteristics in a better position than the other modern forms of retailing to tackle this problem. In fact, several of the measures which may be devised to correct the present state of things, can be taken only within the framework of a department store.

The first step consists in recording the situation and in determining the seasonal, daily and hourly fluctuations of the activity of the personnel (mainly the selling staff). The best unit of measurement is probably the number of transactions per salesman and per hour. Any such investigation reveals a position which in industrial management would be considered as appalling[18].

The measures to improve this situation may be grouped under two different headings: first, those likely to reduce

[17] F. Clark: "Principles of Marketing", New York 1936, p. 236.
[18] See J. Hirsch: "Den moderne Detailhandels Hovedproblemer", Copenhagen 1940, p. 63.

the size of fluctuation in the flow of customers. One may note among them the following: scheduling sales promotion events so as to revive the trade in the dull periods; the reduction of store-wide or divisional sales events in favour of departmental sales events; attempts to influence the shopping habits of customers by the granting of certain privileges if they make their purchases during the dull hours of the day, etc.

A second possible approach to the solution of the problem is by means of measures likely to better the adjustment of the sales force to the fluctuations of the flow of customers. Among the means which may be used to achieve this are the following: the increased use of part-time sales assistants; the use of temporary sales staff; transfer of sales people from department to department; the use of a flying squad of sales assistants; the use of sales staff for non-selling jobs during the slack periods; and the use of the non-selling personnel on the selling floor during the peak sales periods.

Many of these measures are of such a character that they cannot be used to the same extent by unit price stores and specialty chains. This fact alone would be sufficient to warrant a greater attention to this problem.

The question of the utilization of the personnel has been treated in this paragraph from the quantitative point of view; but this question may also be treated from another angle, the qualitative angle. Here one must expect a continuation and a refinement of the application of the principle of the division of labour made with the aim of utilizing the expensive sales assistants' time only for the most productive work. This involves a transfer of the part of their job which can be carried out as well by less skilled workers to other employees, receiving a smaller salary, or the performance of these jobs in centralized non-selling departments where advantage may be taken of the savings resulting from large-scale production and from the use of specialized equipment.

The recent development of pre-selection and of semi-self-service selling has also to be considered as an opportunity for extending that division of labour within the sales force group itself, in the form of a better adaptation of the quality of the personnel to the grade of job. Thus a greater differentiation will be made between the salesmen, with a concentration of the most qualified in those sections and jobs where the customer is supposed to rely on the assistant from the beginning to the end of the transaction, and the use of less qualified salesmen in the sections where semi-self-service selling is in use.

Finance and accounting

In this field department stores will have in the years to come to follow the new conceptions according to which accounting is developed into a tool of analysis rather than used as an instrument of mere historical record, mainly conceived for the needs of the auditor and of taxation.

Some progress has already been made. Thus in the course of these last decades effective means of inventory control have been introduced in a great number of department stores. Furthermore, in expense accounting, the centre of gravity has been shifted from a mere analysis of expenditures to the control of functions and operating units.

The next requirements are a further application of the advanced techniques of modern cost accounting, with a corresponding recognition of definite processes, the development of units of production, the determination of unit costs and of standards, and the introduction of the concept of marginal costs[19]. The application of this scheme may require a reorganization of the department store not only on the administrative side but also on the selling side, so as to have an organization composed of more homogeneous units (departments) from the point of view of their processes of work or of their methods of selling.

The real needs of the modern department store in this field will be met when accounting helps to check the effects of given policies; to explore the consequences of proposed changes in policies; to segregate, in the operating results, the effects of changes in price levels; to test the efficiency of different departments and of different methods

---

[19] See V. Villadsen: "The application of the principle of marginal cost in department stores", Paper presented at the Eighth International Management Congress, Stockholm, 1947.

of selling; and, more generally, to assist the management in its task of finding out the most effective way of organizing the various factors of distribution.

As to the equipment employed, one may note the increased use of modern accounting machines. On the other hand, statistical machines have, until now, been introduced into only a few department stores. Their general use for the accounting and recording work of department stores seems to be awaiting the development of more advanced systems, making it possible to punch the statistical cards conveniently on the very spot where the transactions to be recorded are taking place. This development, together with the possible application of the resources of electronics, will not only mean a rationalization of accounting and recording work but may also open new possibilities for research which would rework at smaller cost the data already prepared for accounting in a form suitable for further re-handling.

Research

At a time when commercial research and management research are becoming factors of growing importance, department stores cannot hope to maintain their place in the economic world without providing for themselves, under one form or another, the services of these relatively new disciplines.

They need to have expert men engaged in the task of watching and appraising the latest developments in a number of increasingly specialized fields and of studying their bearing on department stores.

The executives of a department store are usually too absorbed in the day-to-day operation of their enterprise to devote enough time to the critical examination of their present operating practices, to the development of better operating methods and to the interpretation of economic and social trends.

There is thus a need for a special staff agency represented by a research department in any store whose size is large enough to warrant the creation of such an organ, in any store, say, whose total employment reaches 1,000 people.

Of course, in such a field as retailing the intuition of executives, that ability which Professor Dimock has defined as combination of past experience with an aptitude to form a connection between complicated factors, will always play a great, one may even say a dominant, rôle. But the very progress of management, of business economics and of statistical analysis, as well as the growing complexity of the modern world, make it increasingly necessary to supplement the judgment of the executives by systematic study and, where measurable facts are available, by research.

It is true that the field of distribution is one where intangible elements play a great rôle. Furthermore, the multiplicity of the factors involved, of the motives and, in the case of a department store, of the articles carried, makes the use of the scientific approach difficult. Simple relations of cause and effect are hard to detect, as changes and results in that field are usually the consequence of the action not of one factor but of a combination of factors. And in addition one has rarely the same combination of factors acting twice over. The wide assortment of department stores, the great variety of articles, complicates any job of market research by constantly introducing the disturbing factor represented by multiple alternatives. In management research, the lack of the repetitive factor, or the fact that this factor does not present itself in the same absolute form as in many production jobs, also serves to complicate the task of the research man.

Furthermore, in production jobs the effects of changes introduced for the sake of experimentation or improvement are easier to judge, because the yardstick used to measure the effect is cost, for example the unit cost before and after the change. But in distribution, where the paramount factor is not cost but the volume of sales, any experimentation—for example a change in the layout or the equipment of a selling department—has to be measured in terms of increased sales. And this, contrary to cost, is an element which at any given time will be influenced by a great number of other factors.

One may mention here that from this special angle, the chain of department stores and in particular the chain store (variety chain or specialty chain), which operates several stores in the same locality, is at an advantage, since it can to a certain extent carry out controlled experiments. It can experiment in one store with one factor, the variable to be tested—for example a new arrangement, a given type of display, a new selling method—while keeping this factor unchanged in its other stores. The difference in sales between the branch where the experiment takes place and the other branches of the group may be interpreted as due to the action of the variable which has been tried out, especially if the stores are located in the same town.

The possibilities of research in the field of distribution are more limited than in the field of production. But the need for research is as great in that field as in any other. It is during these last two decades that the resources of modern statistical analysis with its study of variations and its application of the theory of probability have come to the help of distribution. They make it increasingly possible to deal with intangible elements and unforeseeable variables, or at least to limit their disturbing influence.

In its wider aspect, commercial research may be carried out by department stores in order to discover the place of their form of enterprise in the present-day market, to determine what has been the rôle and the function of the department store in the past and in what measure this rôle, this function, subsists.

Besides this long-range research on a wider plane there is plenty of scope for the work of research departments in other, more immediate, directions, for example in studying the administrative machinery of department stores, especially large department stores, and disclosing opportunities for simplification and improvements. Another field of work is represented by the refinement of the tools of management, of the instruments of information and control, placed at the disposal of the executives.

There is also a wide field for research departments in commercial research proper[20]. We have already mentioned

[20] See G. van der Wal: "Un example de recherche appliquée à la psychologie de la clientèle", Bulletin d'information des entreprises à commerces multiples, Paris, July 1953.

the wide variety which characterizes the department stores. Until now the various elements which dominate the operation of department stores—merchandise, suppliers, customers, forms of sales promotion, etc.—have been too much considered in bulk, without any attempt to distinguish within each of these factors, different classes in terms of different degrees of profitability. One of the tasks of research in department stores is precisely to break down the usual operating concepts and figures used in the store, which often represent averages made up of heterogeneous components and which, as such, have little significance, so as to replace them with new concepts based on a more advanced qualitative analysis and, whenever possible, on quantitative measurements. More generally the research department will assist the management in developing the organisation of the firm, its methods and procedures of work, in co-ordinating the activities of the different functions, in appraising results and in correcting unsatisfactory conditions.

VII

CONCLUSION

SINCE this book was written, the war and the post-war seller's markets have come to an end and it is now possible to watch developments in the retail field in a more normal setting.

A characteristic feature of these last years has been the renewed progress of the former unit price stores in the form of the modern variety chains. Whereas the special circumstances of the seller's market were, on the whole, detrimental to that form of distribution by reducing its hold on the supply industry, the resumption of more normal circumstances has once more demonstrated its vigour.

In the food line, a noteworthy development has been the creation or transformation of many food stores into new types of distribution agencies operated on the principles of self-service selling. Furthermore, some of these food stores have reached greater dimensions and represent, in fact, examples of food department stores with the gathering of several different lines of merchandise under one roof.

One may also record one or two recent examples in Europe of supermarkets along American lines, i.e., stores of a relatively large size which offer along self-service selling principles not only different categories of food but also a variety of goods in the textile, hardware and other lines.

These developments are not without danger for department stores, as they tend to take away from department stores a great number of valuable articles, in fact many articles with the highest rates of stockturn; but it may be noted that this expansion nevertheless takes place along lines which in a way vindicate the main characteristic of the department store, namely the gathering of different categories of goods in the same store. At a time when we see a new conception take root, the conception of the shopping centre, it is important to note that the department store has always been and will remain a shopping centre in itself.

This remark is the more important as the specialty chains have, on the whole, not given during these last fifteen years the impression that they represent for department stores the threat which they were supposed to become. We have in this study defined the great forces of modern large-scale distribution as being the concentration of buying power, the opportunity to merge and synchronize the functions of several levels of distribution (for example wholesaling and retailing), and the possibility of using rational methods of research and organization. And the specialty chains appear to be in a better position than perhaps any other form of distribution to use these opportunities. But it seems that this threat has, somehow, not yet materialized. Perhaps this is an example where considerations based on business economics (in this case the importance of the factors: buying power, integration and specialization) are counteracted by some other, psychological and practical, factors, e.g., the difference in the store atmosphere and the greater convenience offered to the customers by stores of larger unit size and by the gathering of different lines of merchandise under the same roof.

As to the department stores, one may note that they have emerged from 10 years of seller's market conditions with some advantages. First of all, the size, the variety of assortment offered in the majority of the departments of a department store had, in the past, tended to be taken too much for granted by the public. This extensive assortment was an element of service to the customer, an element of expense for the store, with the public insisting on it but not showing any real appreciation of its existence. The scarcities of the war and of the post-war period have helped to change that attitude. As a reaction against the standardized assortment and the limited choice of the war and post-war years, the public has attached greater importance to such factors as the variety of assortment and the possibilities of choice, and this reaction has favoured the department stores which have been recognized as stores where the assortment represents a main customer appeal.

The conditions of the seller's market have also served to reduce many exaggerations in the field of sales promotion expenses and customer services. Even now, when normal circumstances are returning, it seems that department stores (at least in Europe) are not yet indulging in the excesses of the 1920's and 1930's. This change of policy is perhaps especially noticeable in the Parisian department stores.

But the problems raised in this study nevertheless remain, and any further strengthening of the buyer's market would make them apparent.

The renewed advance of the unit price stores, the development of self-service food stores (and, tomorrow, of self-service supermarkets offering on self-service principles several lines of goods borrowed from the assortment of the department store) indicate that we are entering upon a phase of retail history in which new influences will be at work, and in which new alignments may take place.

The 20's and 30's have shown us that the department store considered as a form of distribution had reached a point of relative stability and that the increase in total non-food retail sales which took place during these two decades was mainly directed into the newest forms of distribution represented by unit price stores, variety chains and specialty chains.

The time may well have come to reappraise the position of the department store and to defend a position which has been based on the confidence of multitudes of people and which it has taken decades to build[1].

If we take a bird's-eye view of the history of the department stores, we can see that their success was originally based on a number of new factors, such as the offering of goods at fixed and marked prices, the principle of free entrance, the policy of relatively low mark-up and rapid stockturn, the practice of accepting returns, etc. These factors have given to the department store a great advantage, but they had one weakness: they all represented characteristics which other forms of retailing could also adopt and which they have eventually adopted. The department stores then turned to new factors like sales promotion and customer services. These new factors were basically sound. They

---

[1] G. Palmgren, "City", Helsingfors, 1952, No. 1, p. 3.

were in a way even sounder than the earlier ones, as they
represented factors in which the department stores, on
account of their characteristics (large unit size), have an
advantage and which the other forms of retailing cannot
adopt, or at least not on the same scale.

These factors have thus played a great rôle in the expansion of department stores. But they have gradually ex-
hausted themselves by their very exaggeration. The
department store must now find new elements of attraction.
We have listed some of these elements in the preceding
pages. Among these the most suitable are those which
represent an increased use of the opportunities which are
inherent in the department store and which cannot be found
in other forms of retailing.

We have thus reviewed factors like a new departmentalization based on customer needs; a development of creative
merchandising; the greater use of telephone selling mainly
in conjunction with advertising offers; the emphasis on the
fashion factor; and a better and more continuous utilization of the department store based on the opportunities for
combination, transfer and rational timing offered by the
great number of different units composing a department
store.

As to the new form of selling represented by self-service
selling, the department stores cannot adopt it in its most
complete form, i.e., in the form of a combination of self-
selection and of the check-out system. But they certainly
can introduce in several departments, or specific sections, a
greater degree of pre-selection in the sense of a presentation
of the merchandise and of an organization of the selling
in such a way that the forward stock is classified and dis-
played so as to allow the customers to locate the goods,
see the assortment and make their choice (or at least narrow
down their choice), with a smaller or more useful intervention on the part of the sales assistant than heretofore.

This introduction of a greater degree, not of self-service,
but of pre-selection, represents a natural counter-move on
the part of the department store. Under this form, semi-
self-service can be introduced in several sections of a
department store under conditions which do not detract

from the atmosphere of the store but which nevertheless provide most of the advantages of this new form of selling. In fact, there are in a self-service food shop two distinct new elements. The first and the most important is the change brought about in the selling operation proper. The second is represented by the check-out method, i.e., the concentration of the cashiering and packing operations for several purchases in one act. The department store is not interested in the second element, but it can certainly adapt to its needs the advantages of the first.

Viewed from another angle, the policy of using systematically all the potentialities inherent in the department store and all the possibilities it comprehends, leads us to another conclusion. The department stores have been obliged to build an elaborate organization characterized by the fact that they have at their disposal a great amount of commercial and specialized ability in the form of qualified but expensive executives. Under this condition it is often wasteful for the department store to sell mainly the type of merchandise that the small retailer is in a position to carry and sell as well as themselves, and it is also unwise for department stores to concentrate too exclusively on the type of merchandise which the new forms of retailing can handle in more favourable conditions on account of the scale of their operations. One of the purposes of department store policy must in fact be to develop the part of the business where, by the use of the specialized talents at its disposal or its more complete and varied merchandising machinery, it can develop articles or forecast trends better or more quickly than other kinds of retailer or the new forms of distribution.

It is probable that the assortment of a department store must be a delicate combination of two kinds of items. First there are those which the department store carries because it is or wants to become a large enterprise, not only in appearance but in reality, built and organized for size, which is interested (and whose suppliers are interested) in great quantities, long runs, repeat orders. There must be in its assortment some key lines, which are there for volume, for repeat orders, big sales, good terms from the suppliers, competitive prices to the customers, capacity to compete, in comparable articles, with the variety chains. But besides these key lines, the department store must have, in order to remain a department store, a great number of other items which are there to fill in the assortment, to give choice, and also to exploit opportunities. The one aspect of retail distribution that the newest forms of retailing are not likely ever to snatch from the hands of the department stores is leadership in introducing new types of goods.

It may be that on account of this dual approach the department store requires in fact two different kinds of organization and of mind. The first items require the resources of organization, with its systematic character, its somewhat rigid procedures of work. The second items require the flexibility, the power of adaptation, the versatility of the small entrepreneur.

It is not only as regards the articles carried, but also through the methods of operation that department stores must avail themselves of their greater resources, which derive from a more elaborate and refined organization. Thanks to the specialized organs at their disposal they must be the first to determine the various selling expenses of the different kinds of articles or to develop accurate methods of response control for their advertising, and the use of these methods will place them at a distinct advantage over other forms of retailing: they will in fact enjoy the advantage of the business man who can base decisions on evidence as well as on intuition.

In their general commercial practices and in several other fields department stores should again go their own way, as they once did, and learn to develop something that will be both different from the other forms of distribution and characteristic of themselves.

In a world where new ways and especially a new pace of living are gaining ground, department stores may perhaps find an original and rewarding field in offering to the public a commodity which is becoming increasingly scarce, namely time, under the form of time-saving.

New ways of living are rapidly taking root and the department stores would do well to remember that the various things that they offer, that they sell, have in fact always represented a new way of living.

This new field of endeavour may take the form of a re-evaluation of their layout and departmentalization, a change in their opening hours and in their methods of selling, the development of specific lines of merchandise, the creation of additional services (but carried out on a paying basis), all these moves being orientated towards the needs and the problems of the modern customer whose life is increasingly a fight against time.

But in order to be consistently followed, such a direction will necessitate the abandoning of several traditions and ways of thinking, as well as the mustering of plenty of imagination.

It must be at any rate a warning for department stores that pre-selection and semi-self-service selling, which by their implications on salesmanship and, one may add, on commercial morality, probably represent the greatest single innovation in the field of retailing since the suppression of bargaining through the introduction of fixed and marked prices, did not originate from the department stores but from a different source.

Our modern society is undergoing an evolution towards organization, mechanization (and this not only in the material sense of the word), standardization, time-saving and streamlining, which is recognizable in almost every field. The variety chains, the supermarkets and the self-service stores are the representatives of this tendency in the field of distribution.

The department store cannot ignore this change and will have to adapt certain aspects of its operation to the trend. But by doing so it must be careful not to impair its particular atmosphere which will always remain its main appeal. And this because a department store is not merely a place where people come to buy, but also a place where people come to enjoy themselves, to inform themselves, to meet friends—a place, in short, which in certain respects is for the customers an extension of their own homes and not simply a selling machine.

Department stores must thus learn to find new factors of customer attraction and new methods of operation, in order to mould them to their own needs but without sacrificing the definite atmosphere which remains, together with their greater unit size, their main asset.

In fact, their basic problem remains the same as throughout their history: how to reconcile industrial organization with personal service.

>■■►I >■■►I >■■►I >■■►I

SELECTED BIBLIOGRAPHY

ENGLISH

Appel, J. H.: The business biography of John Wanamaker, founder and builder; America's merchant pioneer from 1861 to 1922.
New York, 1930.

Beasley, N.: Main street merchant: the story of the J. C. Penney Company.
New York, 1948.

Beckman, Theodore N.: The chain store problem.
New York, 1938.

Bloomfield, D.: Trends in retail distribution.
New York, 1930.

Brann, W. L.: The romance of Montgomery Ward and Company.
New York, 1929.

Bullock, Roy J.: The early history of the Great Atlantic and Pacific Tea Company.
Harvard Business Review, April, 1933.

Burnham, E.: The department store in its community.
Harvard Business Review, 1940.

Claeson, G.: Retail trade in Great Britain.
Paris, 1938.

Copeland, M. T.: Some present-day problems in distribution.
Harvard Business Review, April, 1931.

Darby, W. D.: Story of the chain store.
New York, 1928.

Ditchett, S. H.: Eaton's of Canada.
New York, 1923.

Ditchett, S. H.: Marshall Field and Company, the life story of a great concern.
New York, 1922 (also German edition).

Dolva, Wenzil K. and Beckley, Donald K.: The retailer: the rôle of modern retailing in the United States.
New York, 1950.

Emmet, B.: Department stores.
Stanford, 1930.

Emmet, B. and Jeuck, J. E.: Catalogs and counters, a history of Sears, Roebuck and Company.
Chicago, 1950.

Filene, Edw. A.: More profits from merchandising.
Chicago. 1926.

Filene, Edw. A., Gabler, W. K. and Brown, P. S.: Next steps forward in retailing.
New York, 1937.

The Filene Book: Wm. Filene's Sons Company.
Boston, 1923.

ENGLISH (*continued*)

Gibbons, H. A.: John Wanamaker. 2 volumes.
New York, 1926.
Golden Book of the Wanamaker stores: Jubilee Year, 1861-1911. 2 volumes.
Philadelphia, 1911.
Hall, M.: Distributive trading, an economic analysis.
London, 1949.
Harvard Bureau of Business Research: Operating expenses of department stores and departmentized stores.
Cambridge, Mass. (Yearly).
Hess, M.: Every dollar counts, the story of the American department store.
New York, 1952.
Hirsch, J.: Standard figures of Scandinavian distribution.
Copenhagen, 1938.
Hower, R. M.: History of Macy's of New York, 1858-1919: chapters in the evolution of the department store.
Cambridge, Mass., 1943.
Hower, R. M.: Urban retailing 100 years ago.
Bulletin of the Business Historical Society, December, 1938.
Hungerford, Edw.: The romance of a great store (Macy's).
New York, 1922.
Hypps, F.: The department store—a problem of elephantiasis.
Annals of the American Academy of Political and Social Sciences, 1936.
Jefferys, J. B.: The distribution of consumer goods.
Cambridge, 1950.
La Dame, M.: The Filene store.
New York, 1930.
Lebhar, G. M.: Chain stores in America, 1859-1950.
New York, 1952.
Lebhar, G. M.: The chain store—boon or bane?
New York, 1932.
Levy, H.: The shops of Britain. A study of retail distribution.
London, 1948.
Marshall: Industry and trade.
London, 1919.
Marshall and Snelgrove, a family of shops.
London, 1951.
Mayfield, F. M.: The department store story.
New York, 1949.
Mazur, P. M.: Is the cost of distribution too high?
Harvard Business Review, October, 1925.
Mazur, P. M.: Principles of organization applied to modern retailing.
New York, 1927 (also German edition).

ENGLISH (*continued*)

McNair, M. P.: Trends in large-scale retailing.
 Harvard Business Review, October, 1931.
McNair, M. P.: The future of the department store.
 "Stores", New York, May 1950.
McNair, M. P., Teele, S. F. and Mulhearn, F. G.: Distribution costs:
 an international digest.
 Boston, 1941.
Nystrom, P. H.: Economics of fashion.
 New York, 1929.
Nystrom, P. H.: Economics of retailing. 2 volumes.
 New York, 1930.
Nystrom, P. H.: Chain stores.
 Washington, D. C., 1930.
Nystrom, P. H.: Retail store operation.
 New York, 1937.
Parnes, L.: Planning stores that pay.
 New York, 1948.
Pasdermadjian, H.: Management research in retailing.
 London, 1950.
Penney, J. C. (as told to Robert W. Bruère): J. C. Penney, the man with
 a thousand partners.
 New York, 1931.
Pfanner, J. A.: A statistical study of the drawing power of cities for
 retail trade.
 Chicago, 1940.
Phillips, Ch. F.: A history of the F. W. Woolworth Company.
 Harvard Business Review, January, 1935.
Phillips, W. B.: How department stores are carried on.
 New York, 1905.
Reilly, W. J.: The law of retail gravitation.
 New York, 1931.
Reilly, W. J.: Methods for the study of retail relationships.
 Austin, Texas, 1929.
Retail Distributors' Association: Operating costs of department stores.
 London (yearly).
Retailing. Productivity team report. Anglo-American Council on
 Productivity.
 London, 1952.
Selfridge, H. G.: The romance of commerce.
 London, 1923.
Smith, H.: Retail distribution, a critical analysis.
 London, 1937.
Tebbel, J.: The Marshall Fields, a study in wealth.
 New York, 1948.
Urwick, L. and Valentine, F. P.: Europe-United States distribution
 problems.
 International Chamber of Commerce, 1931.

BIBLIOGRAPHY

ENGLISH (*continued*)

Wanamaker: The evolution of mercantile business.
Annals of the American Academy of Political and Social Science, 1900.

Weiss, E. B.: Selling to and through the new department store.
New York, 1948.

Wendt, L. and Kogan, H.: Give the lady what she wants (Marshall Field).
Chicago, 1952.

Werner, M. R.: Julius Rosenwald, the life of a practical humanitarian.
New York, 1939.

Wess, H. B.: Profit principles of retailing.
New York, 1931.

Winkler, J. K.: Five and ten: the fabulous life of F. W. Woolworth.
New York, 1940.

Winslet, V. G.: Multiple shop companies.
London, 1943.

Does distribution cost too much? The Twentieth Century Fund.
New York, 1939.

The history and progress of Montgomery Ward and Company.
Chicago, 1925.

The history of Lord and Taylor.
New York, 1926.

FRENCH

Ambrière, F.: La vie secrète des grands magasins.
Paris, 1932.

d'Avenel, G.: Les grands magasins.
Revue des Deux Mondes, Paris, July, 1894.

Bernheim, E.: La distribution des marchandises.
Brussels, 1937.

Carlioz, J.: Le gouvernement des entreprises commerciales et industrielles.
Paris, 1921.

Coets, J.: La structure fonctionnelle des grands magasins.
Brussels, 1944.

Colson, C.: Cours d'économie politique. Volume IV.
Paris, 1909.

Dansette, J. J.: Les formes évoluées de la distribution.
Brussels, 1944.

Duclos, L.: Les transformations du commerce de détail.
Paris, 1902.

François-Cahen, S.: Le grand magasin, baromètre de conjoncture et terrain d'études économiques, Thesis.
Paris, 1952.

Hamery, A.: Les groupements d'achats du commerce.
Paris, 1946.

FRENCH (*continued*)

Jarry, P.: Les magasins de nouveautés, histoire retrospective et anecdotique.
Paris, 1948.

Laguionie, P.: Organisation de la distribution au détail.
Paris, 1938.

Laudet, F.: La Samaritaine, le génie et la générosité de deux grands commerçants.
Paris, 1933.

Leener, G. de: La distribution des marchandises.
Brussels, 1934.

Levasseur, E.: Histoire du commerce.
Paris, 1912.

MacOrlan, P.: Le Printemps.
Paris, 1930.

Mataja, V.: Les grands magasins et le petit commerce.
Revue d'économie politique, Paris, 1891.

Michel, J.: Le commerce en grands magasins.
Revue des Deux Mondes, Paris, July, 1892.

Moride, P.: Les maisons à succursales multiples en France et à l'étranger.
Paris, 1913.

Nogaro, B. et Oualid, W.: L'évolution du commerce, du crédit et des transports depuis cent cinquante ans.
Paris, 1914.

Normand, G.: Le grand commerce de détail.
Paris, 1920.

Paridoc: Les maisons à succursales.
Paris, 1941.

Picard, R.: Formes et méthodes nouvelles des entreprises commerciales.
Paris, 1916.

Pierrefeu, J. de: Contre la vie chère, les magasins à prix uniques.
Paris, 1933.

Pirou, G.: Traité d'économie politique, Volume I.
Paris, 1941.

Reboud, P.: Précis d'économie politique. Volume II.
Paris, 1937.

Sayous, A.: La concentration des entreprises industrielles et commerciales.
Paris, 1913.

Scholer, P.: Le prix de la distribution.
Paris, 1949.

St. Léon, M.: Le petit commerce parisien.
Paris, 1911.

St. Martin, A.: Les grands magasins.
Paris, 1900.

Valmy-Baisse, J.: Les grands magasins.
Paris, 1927.

FRENCH (*continued*)

Zola, Emile: Notes de travail sur les grands magasins.
Oeuvres complètes, Volume 12.
Enquête sur la situation du commerce en France.
Chambre des Députés, session 1914. Journal Officiel 1914.
Documents parlementaires No. 3432.

GERMAN

Blumer-Egloff, J.: Die modernen Grossbazare oder Warenhäuser.
Zürich, 1901.
Denneberg, E.: Begriff und Geschichte des Warenhauses. Privatrecht-
liche Verhältnisse der schweizerischen Warenhäuser.
Zürich, 1937.
Duttweiler: Das Verkaufswagensystem im Lebensmittelkleinhandel.
Zürich, 1926.
Gabler, W.: Volkswirtschaftliche Probleme der Warenhäuser in den
Vereinigten Staaten von Amerika.
Brugg, 1934.
Haase, A.: Der Einzelhandel in Frankreich.
Berlin, 1930.
Hirsch, J.: Die Bedeutung des Warenhauses in den Volkswirtschaften.
Probleme des Warenhauses.
Berlin, 1928.
Hirsch, J.: Der moderne Handel, seine Organisation und Formen und
die staatliche Binnenhandelspolitik.
Tübingen, 1925.
Hirsch, J.: Das Warenhaus in Westdeutschland; seine Organisation und
Wirkungen.
Leipzig, 1910.
Industrie Bibliothek: Hermann Tietz (Volume 31), Karstadt (Volume
36), Brann (Volume 49).
Berlin 1928-1933.
Körner, H.: Die Warenhäuser, ihr Wesen, ihre Entstehung und ihre
Stellung im Wirtschaftsleben, Thesis.
Tübingen, 1908.
Kramer, H.: Warenhausprobleme der jüngsten Zeit.
Leipzig, 1931.
Mazur, P. M.: Moderne Warenhaus-Organisation (edited by F.
Neisser).
Berlin, 1928.
Mutz, R. H.: Das Einheitspreisgeschäft.
Berlin, 1932.
Parnes, L.: Bauten des Einzelhandels und ihre Verkehrs- und
Organisationsprobleme.
Zürich, 1936.

GERMAN (*continued*)

Schliepmann, H.: Geschäfts- und Warenhäuser.
Berlin, 1913.
Schocken, S.: Zwischen Produktion und Konsum.
Berlin, 1931.
Sombart, W.: Der moderne Kapitalismus, 4 Volumes.
Berlin, 1924.
Sombart, W.: Das Wirtschaftsleben im Zeitalter des Hochkapitalismus,
2 Volumes.
Berlin, 1927.
Sombart, W.: Das Warenhaus, ein Gebilde des Hochkapitalistischen
Zeitalters. Probleme des Warenhauses.
Berlin, 1928.
Stresemann, G.: Die Warenhäuser.   Zeitschrift für die gesamte
Staatswirtschaft.
Tübingen, 1900.
Stresemann, G.: Die Wirkung der Warenhaussteuer auf die Industrie.
Berlin, 1902.
Tietz, A. L.: Betriebsformen des Grosseinzelhandels.
Berlin, 1931.
Verband Deutscher Waren- und Kaufhäuser, Probleme des Waren-
hauses.
Berlin, 1928.
Wagner, H.: Ueber die Organisation der Warenhäuser, Kaufhäuser
und der grossen Spezialgeschäfte.
Leipzig, 1911.
Wernicke, J.: Das Waren- und Kaufhaus.
Leipzig, 1926.
Wiener, A.: Das Warenhaus.
Berlin, 1911.
Wüssow, O. von: Geschichte und Entwicklung der Warenhäuser.
Berlin, 1906.
Fünfzig Jahre Leonhard Tietz, 1879-1929.
Cologne, 1929.
Organisation des Warenhauses A. Wertheim.
Berlin, 1907.

DANISH

Hirsch, J.: Den moderne Detailhandels Hovedproblemer.
Copenhagen, 1940.

NORWEGIAN

Schulerud, M.: Fra Krambod til Stormagasin (Steen & Strøm A/S).
Oslo, 1947.

SWEDISH

Damsten, B.: Handelshuset Stockmann genom tre kvarts sekel.
Helsingfors, 1937.
Sachs, J.: Mitt Livs Saldo, Köpman och Förhandlare.
Stockholm, 1949.
Sachs, J.: Varuhuset, en stad i staden.
Stockholm, 1938.
Samuelssson, K.: Nordiska Kompaniet, historien om ett varuhus.
Stockholm, 1952.
Törnqvist, G.: Detaljhandelns Stordriftsformer.
Stockholm, 1936.
Törnqvist, G.: Varudistributionens Struktur och Kostnader.
Stockholm, 1946.

INDEX

GETTING AND SPENDING:
The Consumer's Dilemma

An Arno Press Collection

Babson, Roger W[ard]. **The Folly of Instalment Buying.** 1938

Bauer, John. **Effective Regulation of Public Utilities.** 1925

Beckman, Theodore N. and Herman C. Nolen. **The Chain Store Problem.** 1938

Berridge, William A., Emma A. Winslow and Richard A. Flinn. **Purchasing Power of the Consumer.** 1925

Borden, Neil H. **The Economic Effects of Advertising.** 1942

Borsodi, Ralph. **The Distribution Age.** 1927

Brainerd, J. G[rist], editor. **The Ultimate Consumer.** 1934

Carson, Gerald. **Cornflake Crusade.** [1957]

Cassels, John M[acIntyre]. **A Study of Fluid Milk Prices.** 1937

Caveat Emptor. 1976

Cherington, Paul Terry. **Advertising as a Business Force.** 1913

Clark, Evans. **Financing the Consumer.** 1933

Cook, James. **Remedies and Rackets:** The Truth About Patent Medicines Today. [1958]

Cover, John H[igson]. **Neighborhood Distribution and Consumption of Meat in Pittsburgh.** [1932]

Federal Trade Commission. **Chain Stores.** 1933

Ferber, Robert and Hugh G. Wales, editors. **Motivation and Market Behavior.** 1958

For Richer or Poorer. 1976

Grether, Ewald T. **Price Control Under Fair Trade Legislation.** 1939

Harding, T. Swann. **The Popular Practice of Fraud.** 1935

Haring, Albert. **Retail Price Cutting and Its Control by Manufacturers.** [1935]

Harris, Emerson P[itt]. **Co-operation:** The Hope of the Consumer. 1918

Hoyt, Elizabeth Ellis. **The Consumption of Wealth.** 1928

Kallen, Horace M[eyer]. **The Decline and Rise of the Consumer.** 1936

Kallet, Arthur and F. J. Schlink. **100,000,000 Guinea Pigs:** Dangers in Everyday Foods, Drugs, and Cosmetics. 1933

Kyrk, Hazel. **A Theory of Consumption.** [1923]

Laird, Donald A[nderson]. **What Makes People Buy.** 1935

Lamb, Ruth deForest. **American Chamber of Horrors:** The Truth About Food and Drugs. [1936]

Lambert, I[saac] E. **The Public Accepts:** Stories Behind Famous Trade-Marks, Names, and Slogans. [1941]

Larrabee, Carroll B. **How to Package for Profit.** 1935

Lough, William H. **High-Level Consumption.** 1935

Lyon, Leverett S[amuel]. **Hand-to-Mouth Buying.** 1929

Means, Gardiner C. **Pricing Power and the Public Interest.** [1962]

Norris, Ruby Turner. **The Theory of Consumer's Demand.** 1952

Nourse, Edwin G. **Price Making in a Democracy.** 1944

Nystrom, Paul H[enry]. **Economic Principles of Consumption.** [1929]

Pancoast, Chalmers Lowell. **Trail Blazers of Advertising.** 1926

Pasdermadjian, H[rant]. **The Department Store.** 1954

Pease, Otis. **The Responsibilities of American Advertising.** 1958

Peixotto, Jessica B[lanche]. **Getting and Spending at the Professional Standard of Living.** 1927

Radin, Max. **The Lawful Pursuit of Gain.** 1931

Reid, Margaret G. **Consumers and the Market.** 1947

Rheinstrom, Carroll. **Psyching the Ads.** [1929]

Rorty, James. **Our Master's Voice:** Advertising. [1934]

Schlink, F. J. **Eat, Drink and Be Wary.** [1935]

Seldin, Joseph J. **The Golden Fleece:** Selling the Good Life to Americans. [1963]

Sheldon, Roy and Egmont Arens. **Consumer Engineering.** 1932

Stewart, Paul W. and J. Frederic Dewhurst. **Does Distribution Cost Too Much?** 1939

Thompson, Carl D. **Confessions of the Power Trust.** 1932

U. S. National Commission on Food Marketing. **Food From Farmer to Consumer.** 1966

U. S. Senate Subcommittee on Anti-Trust and Monopoly of the Committee on the Judiciary. **Administered Prices.** 1963

Waite, Warren C[leland] and Ralph Cassady, Jr. **The Consumer and the Economic Order.** 1939

Washburn, Robert Collyer. **The Life and Times of Lydia E. Pinkham.** 1931

Wiley, Harvey W[ashington]. **The History of a Crime Against the Food Law.** [1929]

Wright, Richardson [Little]. **Hawkers and Walkers in Early America.** 1927

Zimmerman, Carle C[lark]. **Consumption and Standards of Living.** 1936